MW00483626

GENDER ON ICE

A M E R I C A N C U L T U R E

Cutting across traditional boundaries between the human and social sciences, volumes in the American Culture series study the multiplicity of cultural practices from theoretical, historical, and ethnographic perspectives by examining culture's production, circulation, and consumption.

Edited by Stanley Aronowitz, Nancy Fraser, and George Lipsitz

American Culture • Volume Ten

GENDER ON
ICE

American Ideologies of Polar Expeditions

LISA
BLOOM

University of Minnesota Press
Minneapolis
London

Copyright 1993 by the Regents of the University of Minnesota

All rights reserved. No part of this publication may be reproduced, stored in a retrieval system, or transmitted, in any form or by any means, electronic, mechanical, photocopying, recording, or otherwise, without the prior written permission of the publisher.

Published by the University of Minnesota Press
2037 University Avenue Southeast, Minneapolis, MN 55455-3092
Printed in the United States of America on acid-free paper

Library of Congress Cataloging-in-Publication Data

Bloom, Lisa.
    Gender on ice : American ideologies of polar expeditions / Lisa Bloom.
        p. cm.—(American culture ; v. 10)
    Includes bibliographical references and index.
    ISBN 0-8166-2091-1 (hc : alk. paper).—ISBN 0-8166-2093-8 (pbk. : alk. paper)
    1. North Pole—Discovery and exploration.   2. United States—Popular culture.   3. Feminist criticism.   I. Title.
II. Series: American culture (Minneapolis, Minn.) ; v. 10.
G620.B54   1993
910'.9163'2—dc20
                                          92-40916
                                           CIP

The University of Minnesota is an
equal-opportunity educator and employer.

For R.R.

Contents

Preface and Acknowledgments

At a time when the United States is renewing its ties to its own imperial past and making peace with itself, it becomes imperative to review certain *gendered* constructions and expressions of its national identity from early twentieth-century popular culture that government officials and the media are seeking to revive today. *Gender on Ice* examines the powerful and continuing cultural investment in the legacy of the so-called discovery of the North Pole in 1909 and the ongoing celebration of "great" white explorers such as Robert Peary as "heroes" of the national culture. This study documents the persistence of this legacy into the present in its examination of a wide range of discourses drawn from popular science magazines, promotional documentaries, science reports, photographs, and novels.

Working within a tradition of cultural studies, deriving a major inspiration from Donna Haraway's *Primate Visions* and Edward Said's *Orientalism, Gender on Ice* takes what might seem a very localized subject and shows how it opens up all the central questions today in cultural studies around gender, nationhood, the politics of imperialism and postimperialism, race and male homosocial behavior, and the social relations of science. The book is also intended to be a contribution to current debates around multiculturalism regarding the definition of what is "American" and who is "American." Thus, in my focus on Matthew Henson, the black American who accompanied Peary to the so-called North Pole, I critique the forms of nationalism endorsed by official U.S. histories that systematically exclude men and women of color. My project will add another dimension to this discussion, as there has been relatively little work on examining the relation between national identities, gender, science, U.S. imperialism, and popular culture. This study challenges official definitions and constructions of U.S. national identities as exclusively white and male. My work brings together scholarship in the humanities (ethnic studies, history of photography, literature, and women's studies) and the social sciences (anthropology and history of science); theories of discourse as elaborated by Michel Foucault and Fredric Jameson; studies of travel and colonialism (James Clifford, Peter Hulme, Mary Pratt, Bruce Robbins, Edward Said); theories of nationalisms (Benedict Anderson, Paul Gilroy, Homi Bhabha, George Mosse, and Gayatri Spivak); gay and postcolonial studies (Richard Dyer, Kobena Mercer, and Simon Watney), and feminist approaches to gender, homosocial relations, technology, and colonialism (Cynthia Enloe, Donna Haraway, Susan Jeffords, Caren Kaplan, Anne McClintock, Chela Sandoval, Eve Sedgwick, Lynne Segal, and Ella Shohat).

The purpose of the book's project is also to put a feminist analysis to work on U.S. nationalism and colonialism, an area that has only recently taken into account the workings of gender, as in the anthology *Nationalisms and Sexualities*. Although earlier texts such as Benedict Anderson's *Imagined Communities* and Homi Bhabha's collection *Nation and Narration* have widened the field of discourse on nationalism in the past decade, what is absent from their theory is an understanding of the way that nationalist events are tied to broader questions of gender. The book makes an intervention by foregrounding these connections in the way that it links the imperial gesture of polar exploration to questions of gender and ties these issues to models of masculinity as well as race.

What follows is a case study rather than a highly theoretical work on the subject of gender and U.S. colonial discourse. Colonial discourse here refers generally to the rhetorical strategies used to manage and control popular scientific knowledges in the course of U.S. expansion and domination. This approach puts emphasis on the ways in which early-twentieth-century discourses are reworked in the context of late-twentieth-century politics. Though the scope of the book is historical, it might prove a disconcerting study for U.S.

historians, for it is written within a tradition of cultural studies that takes as its starting point the political concerns set by the present. It also reverses the trend of traditional history: it deals with gender and race and takes popular culture seriously as its subject of analysis. It is worth pointing out that neither the popular cultural texts nor the literary ones cited in the Introduction are meant to be read as historical or "literary" in a simple sense. They are included as moments of a developing national *colonial discourse*, which I will argue was actually symptomatic of the main trends of U.S. imperialism during the early twentieth century. The study critiques how the North Pole's literal emptiness made polar exploration *appear* in the dominant media as an intrinsically pure field of knowledge rather than as a form of colonial discourse. For example, what was repressed from most media accounts was how the Inuit (Eskimo) people who resided in a nearby region were exploited by polar explorer Robert Peary, who coerced entire Inuit villages to work for him by controlling their trade. The strategies Peary employed to keep the Inuits under his supervision were fairly common colonial strategies, even though they were neither authorized by the U.S. government nor accompanied by a U.S. colonial administration.

The virtual absence of contemporary Inuit accounts has made me more or less exclusively dependent on the very U.S. texts that constitute the discourse of colonialism. Therefore the burden falls upon the rhetorical tools available for critiquing this limited choice of texts. This is very briefly the book's project and focus. Some of the issues that arise from this description are pursued further in the Introduction.

The disregard for the conventional boundaries of disciplinary practices has made me indebted to the advice of both published scholarship and the help of colleagues and friends working in cultural studies.

I am especially grateful for the intellectual guidance and support given by James Clifford. My special thanks to Donna Haraway, who made me attentive to the workings of popular science as well as to the complexity of gender and race relations operating in these texts. Also, I would like to thank Hayden White for working with me over the years and sharing his knowledge.

Professors, colleagues, students, and friends at the University of California, Santa Cruz, provided the critical and the emotional climate to make the work I did possible, and I thank them: Faith Beckett, Victor Burgin, Thyrza Goodeve, Debbie Gordon, Billie Harris, Stephen Heath, Lata Mani, Chela Sandoval, Vivian Sobchack, Elissa Weintraub, and Sara Williams. I owe special thanks to my writing group—Laura Chernaik and Francette Pacteau—for providing editorial guidance and friendship. I am also grateful to my friends outside Santa Cruz for phone calls, encouragement, and intellectual support—Kimberley Flynn, Caren Kaplan, Smadar Lavie, Lisa Lowe, Dana Polan, Irit Rogoff, and Nancy Salzer. I should like especially to thank Roddey Reid, who read the manuscript numerous times and provided encouragement and useful suggestions throughout the duration of this project. Finally, warmest thanks to my family for the affirmation and love that made this book possible: Flora Bloom, Elliott Bloom, Peter Bloom, and Grace Coben.

Introduction

A Passion for Blankness: U.S. and British Polar Discourse

In Joseph Conrad's *Heart of Darkness*, Marlow, while writing about Africa, brings in an unexpected reference to the North Pole:

> Now when I was a little chap I had a passion for maps. I would look for hours at South America, or Africa, or Australia, and lose myself in all the glories of exploration. At that time there were many blank spaces on the earth, and when I saw one that looked particularly inviting on a map (but they all look that way) I would put my finger on it and say, "When I grow up I will go there. The North Pole was one of these places, I remember."[1]

As long as the North Pole remained imperfectly charted and still remote from the knowledge of the West it had a romantic appeal, by the very fact of its blankness on a map. On Marlow's childhood map blankness suspends all the ordinary information that usually makes up geographical space and invites him to reinscribe divisions between nations. It is as if the adult Marlow imagines himself a child with a box of crayons, able to color in the map any way he likes. When it comes to coloring in the blank parts, he will not be subject to the disapproval that any child would hear whose crayon wandered past the edge of France into Germany, or who wanted to divide Poland by coloring it half green and half blue. If he was forbidden to color in the known parts in any way he chose, he was permitted to do what he liked with the blank spaces, which were all brought together to the same plane of representation. The very blankness of these

1

empty parts authorized his access, inviting him to color them in and promising at the same time that he who could begin the process of filling in the blanks was best entitled to possession. Hence, Marlow's fantasy to visit a "particularly inviting blank spot on the map" is constituted by the map, which precedes and legitimizes his desire.

Yet, insofar as Marlow's passion for blankness originated from the document of a colonial map, it was not as "innocent" as suggested by this "childhood" trope. Indeed, Marlow's representation of South America or Africa or Australia as undifferentiated "blank" spaces— pure signifiers without a referent—was only possible within the context of Western colonial expansion. In historical actuality what Marlow refers to as these "many blank spaces of the earth" is not an unrepresentable tabula rasa outside of history or tradition but diverse geographical, historical, and cultural entities. Marking them as "blank" was a discursive strategy that produced the rationale to justify the process of filling them in by the West, through the introduction of Western institutions. Even when blank spaces have been filled, cartographically and discursively, blankness continues to hover in the form of lack attributed to indigenous social formations in need of improvement and reorganization. Theorists of colonial discourse, such as Christopher Miller, contend that it was "European utterances that gave rise to that peculiar empty profile called 'Africa.' "[2] Similarly, Edward Said in his influential book *Orientalism* analyzes the ways in which "European discourses constructed a paper reality which [the Westerner] distinguishes from the brute reality, paper or not, of the Orient itself."[3]

What sets the discursive history of the North Pole apart from the scores of other so-called "blank" spaces on the earth examined by Said and Miller was that the pole was literally empty, making its commercial value rather dubious. Unlike the colonial territories of Africa, South America, or Australia, the North Pole was uninhabited, located not on land but on shifting Arctic pack ice. Yet, as pointless as a trek across a barren wasteland may have seemed to those concerned with financial gain, such an exploit had a pervasive scientific appeal. It literalized the colonial fantasy of a tabula rasa where people, history, and culture vanish. The absence of land, peoples, or wildlife to conquer gave polar exploration an aesthetic dimension that allowed the discovery of the North Pole to appear above political and commercial concerns. Thus, paradoxically, it was the lack of material gain from such an exploit that transformed polar exploration into a new kind of imperial theatre with all its colonial and scientific trappings. The process of erasure characteristic of colonialist texts, however, does reappear in the narratives of polar exploration and discovery, reducing the vital participation of Inuit men and women to subordinate "native bearers" imagined as either "primitive" or "unspoiled" figures.

Expeditions to the North Pole, far from being innocent of the tensions of empire, represented a peculiar stage of colonialism specific to polar discourses that integrated the desire for empire with a presumably disinterested moral and scientific imagination. Dependent upon foot travel and the hard work of "Eskimos," as the Inuit were called, North Polar expeditions were icons of the whole enterprise of colonialism. The complexity of the relation between master and servant in the pursuit of science, however, was consistently written out of the script. Polar explorers with their established network of publications and clubs identified polar exploration as an intrinsically pure field of knowledge, effacing effectively the political dealings with entire Eskimo villages, and the gender and race relations that informed the writings of their texts.

From the mid-nineteenth century onward the successful penetration into "darkest Africa" had left the polar regions as the only large empty spaces on the world map. These last spaces on earth, which still remained invisible and therefore inscrutable, excited a consuming passion on the part of white men of various Western countries to "conquer" and make "visible" these sites. In the narratives of early twentieth-century U.S. and British nationalism, the poles occupy a peculiar position and are a rich source for an analysis of particular imaginary definitions of U.S. and British culture. For England during the years of Pax Britannica, the poles were considered a principal discursive space in which intrepid British naval officers could parade the flag of Britain at the extremes of the planet. Moreover, the literal emptiness of these places served a British imperial fantasy that celebrated empire without the mediating disfigurations associated with the actualities of a colonial state.

The United States was also eager to connect its self-image to the site of the poles. As a tabula rasa, the poles offered an ideal place for the country to establish itself as a great imperial power. In 1903 American explorer Robert Peary tried to convince potential private and governmental backers of the significance of the poles as a mythologized image of U.S. empire:

> Six years ago we were sleeping content within our borders, drowsy of our strength and possibilities. Since then we have embraced the earth, and now right hand clasps left in the far East in a grasp never to be loosened. What a splendid feat for this great and wealthy country if, having girdled the earth, we might reach north and south and plant "Old Glory" on each pole.[4]

Peary's interest in planting Old Glory on each pole occurred at a historical moment when the United States had begun to compete with Europe's empire-building activities.[5] With its success in the Spanish-American War in 1898, the fledgling U.S. empire's boundaries were extended to include new territories—Cuba, Puerto Rico, Hawaii, and the Philippines. The nation's interest in conquering the poles so shortly afterward could be seen as a projection of its expansionist enterprise into an extraterritorial space. Located literally on the boundaries of the world, the poles were thought of as a symbol of the growing strength of the United States. To define and literally to mark the periphery of the world would be a suitable way to reveal the control befitting a nation that aspired to be at the world's center.

Another reason that Peary, who was a civil engineer by profession, placed so much emphasis on the polar conquest was the particular weight such a discovery had in an early-twentieth-century scientific discourse. What it meant to be American at that historical moment was tied into a belief in technology and science. *National Geographic* magazine, a new publication that linked itself to a national image of the United States in the 1890s, seized the poles as a metaphor for modernity and progress. The *National Geographic* presented itself as a new type of geographical literature that utilized photographic representations and advocated exploits that would celebrate the nation's technological achievements. The poles evoked particular interest for the *Geographic* because they provided an example by which new technologies could make what was previously unknown visible to a U.S. readership through a discourse of science. Within the discourse of the *Geographic* the rise of modern science could be called, in Evelyn Fox Keller's words, "the triumph of the visible, its principal goal being clarity, education, the elimination of opacity and the vanquishing of darkness."[6] The *Geographic* affirmed

a discourse that authorized the Victorian view that the West was a superior civilization and that although there might be many stages of
social evolution and many seemingly bizarre customs and supersti-
tions in the world, there was only one civilization, one path of
progress. As a product of that ideology, blank spaces such as Africa
and the North Pole were thought of as places of obscurity until explorers and scientists flooded them with light. The *National Geographic* utilized the photographic record as a means to reveal to a
wider public the latest developments in this drama between light and
dark, a story being reenacted at the ever-receding boundaries of the
earth's periphery. In *National Geographic*, positivist science was understood to be effective at the level of perception itself. Photography
possessed a universally effective revelatory essence. It was the stra-
tegic key that would offer the ordinary reader total disclosure of the
world and its mysteries.

The *National Geographic*'s belief that it can somehow fully explain
what is beyond the horizon of actual vision was used repeatedly as a
motivation for discovering the poles. The ability to make a faithful
record out of what was previously considered imaginary was regarded as a great modern achievement in the early part of the twentieth century. Yet the "faithful record" made at the North Pole was
from the start contested and unstable. In 1909, two U.S. explorers—
Frederick Cook and Robert E. Peary—on different expeditions just
days apart each claimed to have discovered the North Pole. The expedition accounts were purported to contain "information" and
were written in a style of scientific precision. On the trek led by Commander Peary photographs were taken of Peary and his men at the
pole.

At this moment of positivist ascendancy, however, when science
had distinguished itself from fable as the discourse of truth, its findings were open to criticism. Part of the difficulty was that there could
only be one rightful discoverer, and therefore a decision had to be
made to determine which of the two white men deserved the honor.
Paradoxically, the importance given to science alone could not provide a means to determine justly who the winner might be. Calculations were not foolproof, and a photograph of almost any spot could
be made to signify the North Pole by following certain pictorial conventions of the period. To further exacerbate matters exploration accounts by both Peary and Cook that appeared in the *Geographic*

tended to repeat each other in a sort of plagiarizing intertextuality. As a result, determining the true discoverer of the North Pole transformed the conquest of the pole into a spectacle of male rivalry. In the popular press, center stage was occupied not by the pole or by the nonwhite men who did most of the work on the expeditions, but by Peary and Cook, U.S. white men battling for rights of discovery over the most remote region on earth.

Ideologies of gender were central to polar "discovery," and exploration narratives are a rich source for the analysis of stereotypes of white masculinity during this era. In the late nineteenth and early twentieth centuries, polar exploration narratives played a prominent part in defining the social construction of masculinity and legitimized the exclusion of women from many public domains of discourse. As all-male activities, the explorations symbolically enacted the men's own battle to become men. The difficulty of life in desolate and freezing regions provided the ideal mythic site where men could show themselves as heroes capable of superhuman feats. They could demonstrate, in a clichéd phrase of polar exploration narratives, "the boundlessness of the individual spirit." Such claims were hardly likely to accrue to women living within the bounded spaces of everyday life, marriage, and the workplace. The polar explorer represented the epitome of manliness. Men such as these, according to U.S. writer Frank Norris, were destined to rise to power and glory. They could not be held back. A woman might on occasion have dreamed of a life of heroism—as did the female character Lloyd Searight in Norris's *A Man's Woman*—but she would have abandoned her dreams by conforming to the role expected of her sex. Lloyd Searight lives the ideology of her inferiority by sacrificing her work for that of her husband, a polar explorer:

> Was not this her career, after all, to be his inspiration, his incentive,
> to urge him to the accomplishment of a great work?[7]

Even the achievements of women who were Arctic explorers in their own right, such as Josephine Diebitsch-Peary, wife of Robert Peary, were feminized in male accounts to conform more closely to ideals of feminine duty. There was not much of a defined female tradition of exploration, and as a result, many disapproved of Diebitsch-Peary's presence on an Arctic expedition. In part to deflect criticism, Robert

Peary, in his preface to Josephine Diebitsch-Peary's *My Arctic Journal: A Year among Ice Fields and Eskimos*, drew unnecessary attention to her wifely "self-sacrifice" in the Arctic. As he repeatedly put it, her main motivation was to "be by my side" and play a secondary supportive role to him. Accordingly, her status as a woman dependent on her husband is emphasized, ensuring little room for independent action. She would achieve fame as Peary's "nurturing woman" whose presence provided an important source of moral support in *his* effort "to throw more light on the great Arctic mystery."

As white women did not publicly play a role in the Arctic outside traditionally feminine positions, the high regard in which polar exploration was held by male writers such as Frank Norris and Joseph Conrad was not shared by women authors.[8] During this period of polar explorations, Virginia Woolf undercut the unappetizing romanticization of the male polar explorer as a myth naturalizing masculinist supremacy. Her novel *To the Lighthouse* is a critique of a masculinist analytical and objective approach favored by the philosopher Mr. Ramsay, a fictional character she compares to a polar explorer in his pursuit of truth in a straight and orderly course:[9]

> For if thought is like the keyboard of a piano, divided into so many notes, or like the alphabet is ranged in twenty-six letters all in order, then his splendid mind had no sort of difficulty in running over those letters one by one, firmly and accurately, until it had reached, say, the letter Q. He reached Q. Very few people in the whole of England ever reached Q. . . .
> He dug his heels in at Q. Q he was sure of. Q he could demonstrate. If Q then is Q—R—Here he knocked his pipe out, with two or three resonant taps on the handle of the urn, and proceeded. "Then R. . . . " He braced himself. He clenched himself. . . .
> What is R? . . .
> Qualities that in a desolate expedition across icy solitudes of the Polar region, would have made him the leader, the guide, the counselor, whose temper, neither sanguine nor despondent, surveys with equanimity what is to be and faces it, came to his help again. R—[10]

The spatial importance of the alphabet for Woolf is closely allied to its temporal function: Mr. Ramsay climbs tortuously, step by step, toward the truth, whereas Woolf's female characters arrive there in a flash. Mr. Ramsay's slowness and Mrs. Ramsay's more intuitive responses differ greatly, and Woolf couches the difference in explicitly alphabetical terms, as she reflects on

> that old, that obvious distinction between the two classes; on the one hand the steady goers of superhuman strength who, plodding and persevering, repeat the whole alphabet in order, 26 letters in all, from start to finish; on the other the gifted, the inspired who, miraculously, lump all the letters together in one flash—the way of genius.[11]

Woolf is not seduced by an approach to truth such as Mr. Ramsay's or that practiced by polar explorers that favors masculinist modes of rationality. Indeed, she criticizes such a single-minded attention to truth and finds that women's more intuitive and less goal-oriented manner of "lump[ing] all the letters together in one flash" provides a more inspiring example. For Woolf, women did not have to ascend doggedly to the dizzying heights of masculinity in order to prove their genius or heroism.

While Woolf regards women's more intuitive manner of reasoning and men's analytical logic as qualities that are part of the nature of the male and the female, in this book I deal with such attributes as part of a social construction of gender. An extensive literature by feminist theorists has shown that gender identity and ideologies of gender are constructed rather than innate and that these constructions have shifted with changing historical situations.[12] In the early stages of the women's movement, feminist writers were impeded by the ideological assumptions they inherited from nineteenth-century evolutionary biology and anthropology. Feminists naturalized a cultural division that assigned women and human reproduction to the sphere of the natural and the emotive, and men and other human activities to the sphere of the social and the rational.

One of the distinguishing objectives of contemporary feminist criticism has been to de-essentialize constructions of gender, in the process exposing how the biologizing interpretation of history naturalizes women's oppression and makes change impossible.[13] According to Monique Wittig, in order for women to gain control of their lives "women will have to abstract themselves from the definition 'woman' which is imposed upon them."[14] Feminists such as Gayle Rubin have argued that the biological facts—that men have penises

and women do not, that women bear children and men do not—
have no absolute determinate meanings in themselves but are invested with various symbolic meanings by different cultures. Rubin
explains how this process occurs in terms of a sex-gender system—
"that set of arrangements by which biological raw material of human
sex and procreation is shaped by human social intervention."[15]

My project, which deals with questions of race, class, and nationalism as well as gender, has been particularly informed by the shift in
feminist consciousness that has taken place within the past ten years
prompted by recent writings by women of color on race and lesbianism. Since the beginnings of the current feminist movement, and
with particular insistence since the early 1980s, women finding
themselves outside the frame of dominant feminism—lesbians, black
women, other women of color, third-world women—have contested
the terms of its discourse, pointing out the limits of gender as the
sole emphasis and the need for feminists to recognize the claims of
other forms of oppression besides sexual difference. For example,
writers such as bell hooks, Audre Lorde, and Gloria Anzaldúa[16] have
pointed not only to the inadequacies of the prevailing concept of
"woman" as heterosexual and white but also to white feminism's
own consolidation of Western, middle-class interests. In "Sisterhood:
Political Solidarity between Women," an essay appearing in *Feminist
Theory: From Margin to Center*, bell hooks says:

> The vision of sisterhood evoked by women's liberationists was based
> on the idea of common oppression. Needless to say, it was primarily
> bourgeois white women, both liberal and radical in perspective, who
> professed belief in the notion of common oppression. The idea of
> "common oppression" was a false and corrupt platform disguising
> and mystifying the nature of women's varied and complex social
> reality. Women are divided by sexist attitudes, racism, class privilege,
> and a host of other prejudices.[17]

Not only can one not simply add black women to feminist categories, but also according to hooks one must develop a theory that
takes into account the complicity of constructions of gender with ideologies of race and class. The discourse of polar exploration provides
an example of these complex relations, particularly through the hierarchical positioning of white women explorers over "native"
women. Josephine Diebitsch-Peary achieved power over large num-

bers of Inuit peoples in the Arctic from the exaggeration and exploitation of differences of race and nation over differences of gender. Although Josephine may have broken many of the accepted limits of white feminine behavior, she did not confront and challenge any of these restrictions: whatever she achieved outside the traditionally feminine she achieved in part because she was able to benefit from her racial, marital, and national status. Similarly, the discourse of the *Geographic* constructs a narrative drama of masculinity and femininity along lines of race, ethnicity, and nation. In its particular definition of "America," being "American" elevates the status of female readers, for it enables white women to claim superiority over their so-called primitive counterparts and thus to develop a colonial temperament to match their colonial status.

The ways of thinking that inform this book have only been able to surface because of the feminist discussion and scholarship both inside and outside of the university. Particularly valuable to this project has also been the work of feminist critics on masculinities and nationalisms, such as the writing of Susan Jeffords, Cynthia Enloe, Eve Sedgwick, and Donna Haraway,[18] as well as the writings on male sexuality by male activists and by theorists who were influenced by the gay liberation movement.[19] Since the early seventies, questioning and debating masculinity and male sexuality have been integral to the gay movement. The gay perspective has a way of seeing through the rhetoric of masculinity and exposing the emptiness of its images. In part this is because such a perspective threw into relief the ways heterosexual men backed away from the heterogeneous meanings surrounding the sexual domain. Gay male activists and theorists critiqued monolithic definitions in which male sexuality was defined as timeless and unchanging. Theorists such as Arthur Brittan devised terms such as *masculinism* in order not to confuse masculinity with the ideology. Brittan's definition of masculinism is worth quoting at length:

> Those people who speak of masculinity as an essence, as an inborn characteristic, are confusing masculinity with masculinism, the masculine ideology. ... Masculinism takes it for granted that there is a fundamental difference between men and women, it assumes that heterosexuality is normal, it accepts without question the sexual division of labor, and it sanctions the political and dominant role of men in the public and private spheres. ... In general, masculinism

gives primacy to the belief that gender is not negotiable—it does not accept evidence from feminist and other sources that the relationships between men and women are political and constructed nor, for that matter, does it allow for the possibility that lesbianism and homosexuality are not forms of deviance or abnormality, but are alternative forms of gender commitment.[20]

The story of polar exploration raises inescapably the issue of the relation between *masculinism* and *nationalism* in the popular media. As modern nationalism became defined through polar exploration in the early twentieth century, important norms emerged that demarcated ideals of manliness. Theorists of nationalism, such as Benedict Anderson, Paul Gilroy, and George Mosse,[21] illuminate how popular discourses of print and visual media were key features in defining masculinist and nationalist ideologies. Drawing on their writings, I examine homosocial relations as well as the broad process of gender exclusion and racial discrimination that occurs within the domains of discourse and institutional practices that sanction nationalism.

Gender on Ice consists of an introduction and four chapters that compare invidious constructions of gender, race, and class that occur in the United States and England when national ideology is instilled through the mass media. The first chapter examines the story of polar explorer Robert Peary to analyze the workings of a narrative that popularizes U.S. national identity as essentially a white masculine one.

The life of Robert Peary is the stuff of which potent cultural fantasies of science and masculinity were made in the United States in the late nineteenth and early twentieth centuries. Preeminently the myth is associated with Peary's ability to use purportedly scientific methods to map an unknown and forbidding site beyond the limits of a coherent rationality and to make it accessible as an object of science. In the myth of Peary the man and national hero, we are presented with a narrative that heroicized Peary both as the epitome of manliness and as an ordinary practitioner of science who could accomplish the impossible in an age in which recent technological innovations—telephone, cinema, bicycle, automobile, photograph, and airplane—made even the most outlandish scientific exploits seem possible.

In chapter 2 I examine the beginnings of *National Geographic* magazine, an institution that achieved an unparalleled power by, on the one hand, its promotion of a democratic science that it made available to a mass public through the latest advances in photographic technology, and, on the other, partially financing Robert Peary's expedition to the North Pole and legitimizing the venture in terms of a national ideology of scientific progress. *National Geographic* was instrumental in creating Robert Peary as a biographical subject in keeping with the exigencies of a secular hagiography concerned with a certain inscription of the explorer as scientific hero. In my examination of what is missing or repressed from the *Geographic*'s discursive presentation, I reveal how Peary's purportedly scientific methods allowed him to dissociate himself from an old colonial discourse of power and knowledge, including the participation of the expedition's mostly Eskimo work force and single black American, under the guise of a discourse of science. Thus, Robert Peary's expedition promotes a form of nationalism that was fundamentally colonialist in conception but rationalist in expression, representing the Eskimo peoples and an African American man, Matthew Henson, not as exploited workers but as "cogs" that are instrumental in the workings of what Peary termed his well-managed "traveling machine."

A section of the chapter on gender and race relations in the *National Geographic* examines one of the more disturbing "traditions" that the *National Geographic* has upheld—the objectification of the figure of the third-world woman through her eroticization. Photographs of bare-breasted "natives" was one of the ways that the magazine constituted American's national experience as exclusively white and male. The magazine cites native traditions and photographic accuracy as rationales for imposing its gender and race-based concept of the national experience as the dominant one. I align feminism with a critique of positivism in order to analyze the *Geographic*'s colonial discourse of women and development.

The first part of chapter 3 addresses the 1988 National Geographic video special *The Explorers: A Century of Discovery*, which celebrates the National Geographic Society's hundredth anniversary. I focus on how a particular U.S. ideology of science as signified by new photographic techniques that gained its fullest legitimacy in Victorian times still legitimizes the operational protocols of the *Geographic*. I give specific emphasis to the following issues: how the construction of Western vision and point of view intersects with the fashioning of the white, U.S. explorer as universal humanist subject; the role of ahistorical aesthetic concepts such as genius and creativity and how they function as exclusionary terms within a scientific discourse; the persistence of nineteenth-century discourses on white male heroism and science into the present. I examine what happens to white male heroism when the last remaining unexplored regions have vanished and all possible technological means of exploration have been tested and exhausted. I also analyze the major changes that occur when white women and men of color are now included in its contemporary segments as active agents of the institution's discourse.

The second part of the chapter examines past and present contestations and rearrangements of the North Pole story. Focusing on what the *Geographic*'s video narration and its terms omit by repressing social relations, this section examines an account of polar exploration by Matthew Henson, the African American man who accompanied Peary on his polar trek. Henson's account provides a different voice and history than the *Geographic*'s account, which relies for its image on a single white hero playing the active dominant role.

In the fourth chapter on masculinist heroics and myths of empire at the South Pole, I focus on the story of the British polar expedition of Captain Robert Falcon Scott to provide important contrasts and parallels with U.S. polar exploration narratives. I explain how Peary's enterprise of science contrasts with Scott's account, which followed literary conventions and valorized the inner qualities of fortitude and diginity. Drawing on the letters and diaries of those members of Scott's expedition who were denied power by their social position, I activate other sorts of readings of this event. The offscreen disagreements between Scott and his men reported in Roland Huntford's 1979 book *Scott and Amundsen* will be the subject of the second half of this chapter.

I conclude chapter 4 by examining the current reworkings of the Scott and Peary myths. Recent revelations have confirmed my fundamental thesis that both Scott and Peary fabricated the events of their expeditions to suit the particular imperial and masculinist ideologies that each characterized. According to Huntford's revelations, Scott's diaries and letters were altered to turn the official versions of events into something worthy of public reverence. Huntford's reexamination of Scott's diaries reveals that Scott's death was not as orderly and respectable as the heroized version of Scott's journey suggests.

Instead, in the United States Peary is still celebrated as a great man and a hero in the 1988 centennial issue of *National Geographic*, even though one of the articles establishes that he missed the pole by 30 to 60 miles. The continuing anxiety about Peary's credibility manifested itself in findings published in January 1990, which include a 230-page report commissioned by the National Geographic Society that tries to overturn the 1988 admission of Peary's failure and to secure Peary's place once again among the heroes of exploration.[22] Indeed, the *Geographic*'s vested interest in Peary's success does not seem to extend to Henson, who, in this recent report, is still omitted as the co-discoverer of the North Pole. He appears as Peary's "black companion," whose account and participation remain of marginal interest to the *Geographic*'s protocols of national heroism.

1

Nationalism on Ice: Technology and Masculinity at the North Pole

"What sort of a man is Peary?" young Bartlett asked his uncle.
"He's like a T-square, Bob. He thinks in a straight line. And you
can't bend him any more than you can bend steel."

—Robert Bartlett, captain of the *Roosevelt*

On his return from the North Pole in 1909, explorer Robert Peary at his first opportunity sent messages to announce his success. Peary's cables went to the *New York Times*, to the Associated Press, to the secretary of the Peary Arctic Club, and the following to President William Howard Taft:

HAVE HONOR TO PLACE NORTH POLE AT YOUR DISPOSAL.[1]

The president wired Peary in reply:

THANKS FOR YOUR GENEROUS OFFER. I DO NOT KNOW EXACTLY
WHAT I COULD DO WITH IT. I CONGRATULATE YOU SINCERELY ON
HAVING ACHIEVED, AFTER THE GREATEST EFFORT, THE OBJECT OF
YOUR TRIP, AND I SINCERELY HOPE THAT YOUR OBSERVATIONS
WILL CONTRIBUTE SUBSTANTIALLY TO SCIENTIFIC KNOWLEDGE.
YOU HAVE ADDED LUSTRE TO THE NAME "AMERICAN." (65)

According to historian C. D. B. Bryan, President Taft's response was somewhat muted because four days earlier he had received a telegram from Frederick Cook announcing his own attainment of the pole. Taft did not want to commit himself yet to Peary. Moreover, when he writes, "I do not know exactly what I could do with it," he ambivalently refuses to accept Peary's offer of the pole as if it were a trophy delivered to a sovereign. Taft sensed, perhaps, that the pole's discovery was a much mediated process involving forms of power and authority no president could command, forms linked to modern

Robert Peary

technologies of scientific validation and media communication put in the service of a new nationalism at the beginning of the twentieth century.

National Geographic Society, Scientific Controversy, and Robert Peary

Drawing from Michel Foucault's analysis of historical writing, of discursive formations and their practical institutionalization,[2] I will study the textual terrain by which Gilbert Grosvenor and Peary were able to establish a mutually authorizing relationship that promoted a particularly powerful masculinist and nationalist discourse in the United States at the beginning of the twentieth century.

The dissemination of Robert Peary's North Pole exploration narratives during the early part of the twentieth century depended heavily on the institutional formation of the *National Geographic* magazine and its discursive practices.[3] Peary's expeditions were the first to be funded by the National Geographic Society and set a precedent for the type of scientific research that was later sustained by its membership.[4] *National Geographic* also took an active role in securing and protecting Peary's reputation both throughout his career and posthumously. When controversy arose over the conflicting claims of Peary and Frederick Cook to have each gained the pole, an arbitrating committee was appointed by the National Geographic Society. It is significant that the *Geographic*'s decision that Peary was, indeed, the discoverer of the North Pole ended up holding more weight than did the findings of a 1911 congressional committee that struck the words *discover* and *discoverer* from the record. Not only was Peary unable to offer proof of his discovery at the hearing, he admitted that he had taken "no observations for longitude at any time on the trip" and made no observations for compass variation.[5] That the Peary-Cook controversy is still going on after the conclusive findings of the committee is in part the result of the backing of the National Geographic Society and of its ability to impose Peary as both a national hero and an exemplary representative of National Geographic's particular *image* of masculinity, nationalism, and popular science.

Peary's claim was always disputed. Cook, after all, had his allies, but none were as powerful as the National Geographic Society. Not until 1973, when Dennis Rawlins published *Peary at the North Pole: Fact or Fiction?*[6] was Peary's claim seriously challenged in public. Moreover, the challenge did not come to the attention of a broader public until fairly recently. In December 1983, CBS television screened "Cook and Peary: The Race to the Pole," a drama that tried to prove that Cook had reached the pole a year before Peary but had been denied his claim by Peary. As a result of this television drama, it was suggested that the National Geographic Society had perpetrated a fraud upon the public. Gilbert M. Grosvenor, on the *National Geographic* magazine's president's page, responded that the CBS program was "a blatant distortion of the historical record, vilifying an honest hero and exonerating a man whose life was characterized by grand frauds."[7]

The *Geographic* continued to defend the reputation of Peary but eventually shifted its tactics. In its centennial issue of September 1988 the magazine published an article entitled "Did He Reach the Pole?" in which the author, Wally Herbert, a British polar explorer, argued that through a combination of navigational mistakes Peary probably missed the pole by as much as 30 to 60 miles.[8] Herbert based his claim on what he deduced was the team's miscalculation of the westward drift of the ice pack. According to Herbert, "any one of several navigational errors uncorrected during his outward journey could have robbed Peary of the Pole" (413). He then points out that Peary's chronometer—critical in navigation—was ten minutes fast and that Peary was unaware of that error. Perhaps most disturbing is that Herbert shows that Peary did not obtain the essential data he would need to verify his findings. Herbert explains that missing from his account was

a detailed record of wind speed, weather, and ice conditions; a steady progression of position checks by altitudes of the stars, the planets or the sun for longitude and latitude, as well as checks for compass variations along the route. (412)

Herbert's doubts were also raised when he found discrepancies in Peary's North Pole diary. For many years the Peary polar diary has been stored in the National Archives, with restricted access. In 1988 the Peary family agreed to release it, and the Geographic commissioned Herbert to examine the diary. He found the diary disturbing and was unable to explain why Peary made no entries for the dates of his arrival at the pole. Instead, there was an unattached page on which Peary noted, "The Pole at last!!!" (388). Herbert found it incongruous that Peary's diary was missing the record of Peary's activities during the 30 hours he and his companions spent in the vicinity of the pole. Also confusing was the evidence that Peary had left blank his destination on the cover of his 1909 diary. The incomplete inscription reads: "No. 1, *Roosevelt* to——& Return, Feb. 22 to April 27, 1909, R.E. Peary, U.S.N." (388). By referring to this omission, Herbert implies that Peary himself was not certain he had reached the pole:

> He gives the date of his return to land, crosses it out, and puts his return to the ship. Why did he not insert "North Pole," those two words that spelled out his very reason for living? (388)

As damaging as Herbert's refutation of the factual basis of Peary's claim was, he does not dispel the image of Peary as a national hero nor does he question the reputation of the *National Geographic*. Herbert's critique is minimized by his presentation of Peary as a heroic but "fallible" genius. For Herbert, a British explorer, it did not matter that Peary might not have made it to the pole, for "he was a far more human hero than previously realized" (390). Herbert's acceptance of Peary is contingent on framing Peary within a biographic discursive structure, and on designating his failure as merely an "expression" of his "transcendent" and "creative" subjectivity. However, such a presentation of Peary as "genius" and "heroic failure" by a British man working out of a tradition of heroism founded by Scott and his heroic failure at the South Pole did not prove operative in a U.S. context. The National Geographic Society subsequently rejected Herbert's claims in favor of a more recent version.

In January 1988 the *Geographic* commissioned the Foundation for the Promotion of the Art of Navigation, a Maryland-based group headed by navigator Thomas D. Davies, to undertake what resulted in an exhaustive 230-page report intended to put an end to the controversy. In the January 1990 *Geographic* Davies summarized the report's findings.[9] He used Peary's original photographs to argue that Peary's expedition had reached the vicinity of the North Pole in 1909. Photogrammetric analysis by the foundation confirmed that position within five miles. On the basis of this technical proof, Davies tried to invalidate Herbert's criticisms as "anecdotal evidence" of interest only to "historians or psychologists rather than navigators" (60). He further explained that

> Peary's answer to the congressional committee that he was too busy to fill in his diary on certain dates seems credible. He was certainly busy during the 30 hours spent at the Pole . . . and afterward, driven by the need to survive, hastening back to his base as quickly as humanly possible. Keeping a diary must sometimes be secondary to survival. (60)

Here Davies assumes that Peary did not need precise proofs for his claim, implying that his deeds should not have been disputed in the first place. The report concludes by legitimizing the authority of the *Geographic's* older discourse of male heroism over that of scientific accuracy.

The *Geographic's* Image: Hudson, Magellan, Columbus, and Peary

The lengthy passage by *Geographic* editor Gilbert Grosvenor that I excerpt below appeared both in the magazine and as the preface to Robert Peary's official 1910 book, *The North Pole: Its Discovery in 1909 under the Auspices of the Peary Arctic Club.*[10]

As patron, publicizer, and eulogist, Grosvenor in this passage hails Peary as the exemplar for what an "average American" could achieve through U.S. scientific know-how. Peary is affiliated with other great men — "Hudson, Magellan, and Columbus" — and the United States is represented as superior not only to "primitive" non-Western cultures but also to its "civilized" European counterparts (italics throughout the quote are mine):

> *The struggle for the North Pole* began nearly one hundred years before the landing of the Pilgrim Fathers at Plymouth Rock, being *inaugurated (1527) by that king of many distinctions Henry VIII of England.* . . .
> Scores of hardy navigators, British, French, Dutch, German, Scandinavian, and Russian, followed Davis [the first arctic explorer], all seeking to hew across the Pole the much-coveted short route to China and the Indies. The rivalry was keen and costly in lives, ships, and treasure, but *from the time of Henry VIII for three and one-half*

centuries, or until 1882, Great Britain's flag was always waving nearest the top of the globe. ... (xv)

The first half of the 19th century witnessed many brave ships and gallant men sent to the arctic regions. *England hurled expedition after expedition, manned by the best talent and energy of her navy,* against the ice which seemingly blocked every channel to her ambitions for an arctic route to the Orient. ... (xvi-xvii)

No band of men ever set out for the unknown with brighter hopes or more just anticipation of success than *Sir John Franklin's expedition of 1845.* The frightful tragedy which overwhelmed them, together with the mystery of their disappearance, which baffled the world for years ... *forms the most terrible narrative in arctic history.* ... (xix)

The story of the last Peary expedition, which resulted in the discovery of the Pole and of the deep ocean surrounding it, is told in the present volume by Commander Peary. ... (xxi)

In his first north polar expeditions, which lasted for four years, 1898–1902, Peary failed to get nearer than 343 miles to the Pole. ... On the next attempt, *Peary insured reaching the polar ocean by designing and constructing the* Roosevelt, *whose resistless frame crushed its way* to the desired haven on the shores of the polar sea ... (xxxi)

... No better proof of *the minute care with which every campaign was prearranged* can be given than the fact that, though Peary had taken hundreds of men north with him on his various expeditions, he has *brought them all back, and in good health,* with the exception of two, who lost their lives in accidents for which the leader was in no wise responsible. *What a contrast this record is to the long list of fatalities from disease, frost, shipwreck, and starvation* which in the popular mind has made the word arctic synonymous with tragedy and death. ... (xxxi-xxxii)

Thus Robert E. Peary has crowned a life devoted to the exploration of the icy north and to the advancement of science by the hard-won discovery of the North Pole. *The prize of four centuries of striving yielded at last to the most persistent and scientific attack ever waged against it.* Peary's success was made possible by long experience ... and by an unusual combination of mental and physical power—*a resourcefulness which enabled him to find a way to surmount all obstacles, a tenacity and courage which knew no defeat, and a physical endowment such as nature gives to few men.* (xxxii)

It has been well said that *the glory of Peary's achievement belongs to the world and is shared by all mankind. But we, his fellow-countrymen, who have known how he has struggled these many years* against discouragement and scoffing . . . that would have crushed less stalwart shoulders, *specially rejoice that he has "made good at last," and that an American has become the peer of Hudson, Magellan and Columbus.* (xxxvii)

In order that readers would be able to identify with Peary as a great hero, "the peer of Hudson, Magellan and Columbus," Grosvenor's narration exaggerates the international importance of the discovery of the North Pole. He extends the chronology of the quest for the North Pole to include the search for the Northwest and Northeast passages, to make England's participation in "the struggle for the North Pole" appear more significant than it actually was.[11] Britain's dominating presence in the story then enables Grosvenor to locate the rivalry for the pole among the most powerful nations of the age. In this way, the U.S. victory in "winning the prize of four centuries" rhetorically establishes that nation as a great power with an imperial lineage and an Anglo-Saxon tradition. The logic of the narrative suggests that because the United States has won the prize in competition with a great power—England—it too must now be a power of world significance. Peary's discovery thus becomes emblematic of a reversal of global power relations. Moreover, in the course of Grosvenor's narrative Peary and the United States become interchangeable. With the discovery of the pole, a former British colony is transformed into a world superpower, and an ordinary citizen becomes an international hero. Shifts in power relations do not emerge gradually in this narrative. They happen magically. Peary's discovery brings about a complete metamorphosis. At the beginning of the narrative the North Pole is a site of struggle, a source of rivalry among nations. The conclusion not only resolves this tension but transforms the site into a future source of international unity and harmony. Grosvenor's final gesture of offering "the glory of Peary's achievement . . . to the world and . . . all mankind" heralds a new world peacemaker.

The United States liberally bestows its spiritual gifts to those within its borders as well, according to Grosvenor. The ordinary citizen is drawn up and elevated to the realms of higher humanity. The reader is beckoned to identify with Peary, a universal hero but also one of us, "a fellow citizen." We can "specially rejoice" with him that "he has made good at last." Grosvenor's friendly tone expresses the U.S. form of democracy: a democracy in which glory is available for all. Ordinary citizens cannot only identify with great Americans—now international heroes—but can be mythified alongside them.

In Grosvenor's narrative the United States ties itself to European tradition and history, but only to make the nation's own past seem more venerable. As a result of Peary's discovery, the United States establishes for itself a new place connected to European tradition, yet without the mustiness of age. The United States has cleaned away the cobwebs from Europe's past. The success of Peary's "well-arranged" expedition removes the stigma of the Arctic as a site of horror populated with corpses and relics of failed expeditions such as Franklin's. The U.S. claim on the North Pole relegates disease, famine, and other forms of human misery to something of a less than scientific past. As Grosvenor put it, "What a contrast this record [Peary's] is to the long list of fatalities from disease, frost, shipwreck, and starvation which in the popular mind has made the word arctic synonymous with tragedy and death" (xxxii).

It is fitting that Peary, who represents the essence of the United States in the narrative, is depicted as a scientific manager. Peary is the preeminent polar explorer because he is the "most persistent and scientific" (xxxii). "The minute care with which he prearranged every campaign" (xxxi) enables him to overcome the flaws of early polar expeditions. Peary is a practitioner of science, not an innovator. Thus, ordinary persons can identify with him. They, too, can become potent like him by managing the tools of science. The role Peary plays in Grosvenor's narrative is not unlike the position he occupied as civil engineer in the U.S. Navy. Still, Peary also stands as a mythic figure for his fellow citizens, and his alliance with science provides him with an experience that exceeds that of all other men. With such weight given to the role of science in determining Peary's success, it is peculiar that Grosvenor gives little explanation to the details of its workings on Peary's expedition. Although he does not focus on its particular details, he magnifies science's effects. For example, in his description he endows Peary's ship with a "resistless frame" (xxxi).

Though Grosvenor establishes U.S. scientific superiority as essential to this narrative of U.S. identity, surprisingly he points out no contradiction in the narrative when we learn that Peary's technology is not all ultramodern or even derived exclusively from scientific advances made by the United States. Grosvenor's narrative establishes Peary's dependence upon Eskimo culture and technology by explaining how it taught Peary to survive in the region, yet he denies the Eskimos a culture and history except in terms of how their presence in the Arctic regions posed a dangerous threat to earlier European explorers.[12] The Eskimos, however, are no longer considered a violent presence once Peary has arrived on the scene to tame and transform them as a resource for his own purposes. According to Grosvenor the Eskimos both provide a source of new technology and are a technology themselves:

> His experiences ... convinced Peary ... that the only way of surmounting this ... most formidable barrier was to adopt the manner of life, the food, the snow houses, and the clothing of the Eskimos, who by centuries of experience had learned the most effective method of combating the rigors of arctic weather; ... and lastly to train the Eskimo to become his sledging crew. (xxx)

Grosvenor emphasizes Peary's resourcefulness in utilizing both the Eskimos' methods of survival in the region and their labor power for his own purposes. The Eskimos, described as "the best obtainable material for the personnel of a serious Arctic party" (xxx), quickly lose their autonomy as a distinct culture and people and become naturalized as signs of Western industry. As a result, the unequal power relations between the Eskimos and the Americans are suppressed. The terms by which the Eskimos accept their training as part of Peary's "sledging crew" are left out of Grosvenor's narrative.

One of the implicit arguments made in Grosvenor's mythological account is for the universalism of science. Science has a magical effect in the narrative. It transforms everything it touches, making ships unsinkable, and turning ordinary men into supermen. Whatever is problematic is eliminated. Once the regime of science is established, disease and tragedy magically vanish. The belief in science as a solution to the world's problems is so strong that even such diverse groups of people as the Eskimos and the Americans can be brought together to contribute to the "extension of its bounds."

Of course, Peary's discovery of the North Pole was a collective effort. In Grosvenor's official account, the essential group of Eskimo men gets only brief mention as the "sledging crew," and Peary's black American companion, Matthew Henson, who accompanied him to his farthest point of navigation, is completely omitted. Absent, too, is any mention of Peary's rival, Frederick Cook.

Frederick Cook's Defeat by "Unclean Hands"

Frederick Cook's claim to have discovered the North Pole preceded Peary's by one year. But Cook, unable to make it back to so-called civilization directly after his polar discovery, announced his claim just days before Peary announced his own. Cook wrote in his autobiography, *My Attainment of the Pole*, that he believed "there was glory enough for two,"[13] but the various public institutions were determined to decide which of the two men was the true discoverer. A bitter public controversy ensued in which Peary emerged the winner. Robert Peary hardly mentions Frederick Cook in his 1910 autobiography. Yet, Cook writes at length on Peary in his published account:

> Following Mr. Peary's return, I found myself the object of a campaign to discredit me in which, I believe, as an explorer, I stand the most shamefully abused man in the history of exploration. ... With a chain of powerful newspapers, a financial backer of Peary led a campaign to destroy confidence in me. (8-9)

In Cook's autobiography the story of his discovery of the North Pole includes "the story of an unworthy plot" to ruin the reputation of the author:

> I shall tell of a tragedy compared with which the North Pole and any glory accruing to its discoverer pales into insignificance—the tragedy of a spirit that was almost broken, of a man whose honor and pride was cut with knives in unclean hands. (21)

Cook's sensationalized exposure of Peary was a best-seller that went through numerous editions and sold over 60,000 copies. By making the terms of his public suppression visible, Cook was able to turn the celebration around Peary's discovery of the North Pole into a public scandal.

There was no room for such a controversy in Grosvenor's narrative. In his account it is striking that not only is the bitter rivalry between Peary and Cook absent, but there is no mention whatsoever of Cook's 1908 polar expedition. Because both Cook and Peary were Americans, either man could be inserted interchangeably into Grosvenor's narrative as representative of the nation without altering the nationalist thrust of his narrative. The problem was that there were

Dr. Frederick Cook

two separate discoveries and a decision needed to be made to decide which was the rightful one.

Such a confusion around who held the official rights to the North Pole's discovery would be a problem unbefitting a great nation, especially as one of the points of Grosvenor's narrative is that with the discovery of the North Pole, the United States had resolved both U.S. and world tension. In Grosvenor's idealized image of a country united by the discovery of the North Pole there could be no place for unresolved rivalry, especially the national scandal that Cook's prior claim caused.

At the time that Cook announced his polar discovery, he was a well-known polar explorer who had wide experience in both the Arctic and the Antarctic. He was the founder and president of the New York Explorers Club. Before he began his career as an explorer, he went to medical school and received training as a surgeon at the College of Physicians and Surgeons at Columbia University. Robert Peary had given Cook his first opportunity to explore the Arctic, when in 1891 Cook volunteered to join Peary's North Greenland polar expedition as a surgeon. Cook returned with Robert Peary to the Arctic a second time in 1901. Besides the Arctic experience Cook gained through his association with Peary, who was nine years Cook's senior, Cook became involved in a number of other polar expeditions. He was the organizer of a large U.S. scientific expedition to the Arctic in 1893 and was a member of the Belgian Antarctic Expedition of 1898-99 led by the polar explorer Roald Amundsen. In 1900 he published his first book, *Through the Antarctic Night*, which brought him considerable fame as an explorer, anthropologist, and writer on exploration.

Peary's background was different from Cook's. Before he began his polar career in 1886, Peary had received training as a civil engineer and had worked for the U.S. Navy as a surveyor for a canal project in Nicaragua. He made his first trip to the Arctic in 1886 to explore the Greenland ice cap and survey the northeast coast of Greenland. With endorsements from various geographical institutions, including the American Geographical Society, the Brooklyn Institute of Arts and Sciences, the Academy of Natural Sciences of Philadelphia, the National Geographic Society in Washington, D.C., and the American Association for the Advancement of Science, Peary was able to make subsequent trips to Greenland in 1891, 1893-95, 1896, and 1897. Before he began his efforts to reach the pole, his accomplishments comprised the so-called discovery of various land regions near the northeast coast of Greenland, which he named Peary Land, Jesup Land, Cape Thomas Hubbard, and Crocker Land; an exhibition at the 1893 World's Columbian Exposition in Chicago based on his ethnographic study of an Eskimo tribe; and the discovery of meteorites in Greenland that he then transported to the United States. Although maps, encyclopedias, and dictionaries credited Peary at the time for these earlier discoveries, scientists and explorers continued to examine the evidence. As Cook later reported in *Return from the Pole*, in 1916 the U.S. Navy Hydrographic Office removed five of Peary's reported discoveries from government charts (*RP*, 35). Peary Channel, which Peary had described as a waterway running across Greenland from east to west, the explorer Knud Rasmussen showed did not exist; the Danes found no land where Peary had charted Crocker Land and Jesup Land. As late as 1950 Peary's land claims were still refuted. A. G. Anderson, head of the U.S. Navy Hydrographic Office, wrote: "Crocker Land, which Peary thought he observed . . . is now generally believed not to exist" (*RP*, 35).

When he embarked on his 1909 polar expedition, Peary was a reputable polar explorer who had led seven Arctic expeditions during a period of twenty-three years. For his final polar trek, Peary had the endorsement of President Theodore Roosevelt, the support of the U.S. Navy, and the sponsorship of the National Geographic Society in Washington and the American Museum of Natural History in New York. Although high governmental officials had encouraged Peary's project, private institutions financed it. In 1899 the Peary Arctic Club was formed with the express purpose of backing Peary's explorations. The thirty-one members of the Peary Arctic Club included magnates of the Colgate Soap Company, the U.S. Steel Corporation, the Atlantic Mutual Insurance Company, and the Bankers Trust Company.

The support of the Peary Arctic Club was a fundamental factor in the Cook-Peary controversy and its ultimate outcome. The elite circle of millionaires that made up the club contributed a total of $350,000 toward Peary's 1909 expedition and apparently did not take lightly Cook's intrusion into their program. Referring to the fight against Cook, Herbert Bridgman, the secretary of the club, was quoted as stating that they would spend "a half million, if necessary, to see Peary through."

Cook began to formulate other plans to satisfy his own polar ambitions when he first learned that Peary was organizing an elaborate expedition to conquer the North Pole. In an article entitled "Why Not Conquer the South Pole?" Cook wrote in 1907:

> The Boreal Center has managed to hold public interest. The Austral point has been neglected. Why? Great enterprises depending upon popular acclaim for financial support drift with public opinion in narrow grooves. . . . To the South Pole, to the new fairy land of scientists! This should be the foreword of coming explorers. It is a problem peculiarly adapted to American dash, and it should be achieved under the Stars and Stripes. (11)

Cook's earlier interest in the South Pole, however, never gained the support that he needed. He planned his North Polar expedition informally and received support from only one friend, the millionaire John R. Bradley. Cook's plan was to accompany Bradley on a hunting trip to the Arctic, and if conditions were favorable he would remain to make an attempt to reach the pole the following year. When Cook left in Bradley's boat from Gloucester, Massachusetts, in July 1907, it was believed that he and Bradley were off to hunt bear and walrus in the Arctic region. Not until Bradley arrived in New York in the late fall of 1907 with a letter from Cook to the Explorers' Club was the full extent of his plan known:

> I find that I have a good opportunity to try for the pole, and therefore, I will stay here for a year. I hope to get to the Explorers' Club in September 1908 with the record of the pole. . . . Here's for the pole with the flag. (12-13)

Reaction among Peary's supporters to Cook's announcement was one of indignation. Herbert Bridgman, secretary of the Peary Arctic Club, expressed the sentiments of the Peary group:

> The fitting out of the *Bradley* by stealth, while within the prescriptive rights of the owner, invited remark among men who respect honor and observe fair play. . . . That his [Peary's] men, methods, and reasoning should be appropriated and the long struggle finished before he had his fair and final opportunity is a transaction upon which the American people will render just judgment. (13)

Although Peary supporters suspected Cook would fail, they were still concerned that Cook would cheat Peary out of his victory. Determined to protect his interests, upon Cook's return Peary chose as the arbitrator in the controversy the National Geographic Society in Washington, which had published accounts by the Peary Arctic Club and had been one of the financial backers of his 1909 expedition. Peary might have let the verdict be decided by the National Geographic Society alone. But he wanted to be named a rear admiral in the U.S. Navy and receive a retirement salary of $6,500 a year. The appointment required approval by Congress. In January 1911, Peary appeared before the congressional committee to prove his polar discovery. He admitted that the only examination of his instruments ever made by the National Geographic Society had taken place "after dark" in the baggage room of the railroad station where he had his trunk. In addition, he claimed that the inspection did not include a check on the accuracy of his instruments.[14] There was no new inspection of his instruments at the congressional hearing, either. The only proof he offered was his word. Peary was unable to persuade Congress, even with the backing of the president, the secretary of the navy, and the the National Geographic Society, that he had discovered the North Pole. Significantly, the words "discovery" and "discoverer" were stricken from the bill that had been introduced at the request of the National Geographic Society (*RP*, 33). After the hearing, Peary was still recognized as a notable Arctic explorer. He was granted his retirement pension from the Navy. He received medals in the United States and Europe—in most cases not for discovery of the pole, but for "Arctic services" and "for Arctic exploration" (18).[15]

Despite the damaging report of the 1911 congressional committee, Peary's reputation was not compromised. In 1920 he was buried at Arlington National Cemetery and honored as a U.S. hero. Inscribed on the monument placed upon his grave by the National Geographic Society was Peary's motto, "I shall find a way or make one," and a legend honoring him as "Discoverer of the North Pole." His casket was draped with the remnants of the Stars and Stripes with which he had wrapped his body on the Arctic expeditions.

Cook never received any monetary rewards or official polar honors. When he brought his case in front of five scientists at the University of Copenhagen, the jury had no other recourse but to bring down a verdict of "Not Proven" because he was unable to produce his instruments or original field calculations. Cook had left his instruments and original records of astronomical observations with Harry Whitney, a member of the New York Explorers' Club who had been sent to meet Cook on his return from the pole. Peary refused to permit Whitney, who was scheduled to return on Peary's ship, to bring Cook's records, scientific instruments, and other property on board. Whitney put Cook's property in boxes and buried it in the rocks of Etah, where Peary's boat was anchored. The cache was never recovered, and Whitney observed on his return to the United States:

> Ten years ago Peary did with the explorer Sverdrup, who was cruising in Smith Sound, what he had done with Cook: he refused to bring back any of Sverdrup's letters and records. (43)

Cook's inability to furnish proof of his discovery was a significant factor in the controversy that resulted in the eventual ruin of Cook's reputation as a polar explorer. After 1910 Cook led a rather precarious existence. He made an anthropological expedition to Borneo, served as a geologist in Wyoming, and then became an oil promoter in Fort Worth, Texas (43). There, in 1923, he was convicted for misrepresentation, fined $12,000, and sentenced to fourteen years and nine months in a federal penitentiary—the longest sentence on record for this crime. He was also accused of using the mails to promote "worthless" stock in the Petroleum Producers' Association, of which he was president. The case received wide publicity, with Cook insisting that he was innocent, and that he had sold the stock in good faith.

Cook was sentenced in November 1923. His appeal was denied, and he was sent to Leavenworth in April 1925, with no time allowance for months spent in jail. An exemplary prisoner, Cook assisted in the hospital, organized a night school, and edited *New Era*, the Leavenworth Penitentiary paper. He was paroled in March 1930.

The oil lands of Cook's company, declared almost valueless by the government, were bought by an oil company at the U.S. Marshal's sale, and one parcel purchased for $10,000 brought in millions while Cook was still in Leavenworth. Cook wrote to *Time* magazine in 1936:

> I was tried and convicted for overstating potential values in prospective oil fields. . . . The potential oil lands which I had acquired were not fully tested and were stamped as practically worthless by the prosecution. It is a fact, and this has not been

reported by those who have tried to defame me, that some of the lands under question have since produced wealth of millions, far beyond the wildest assertions which I made in literature and letters of the company. (44)

Between 1930 and 1935 Cook wrote *Return from the Pole* and declared: "Before I die I must clear my good name" (45). He suffered a cerebral hemorrhage on May 3, 1940. Two weeks later Franklin D. Roosevelt pardoned him, restoring his civil rights. He died on August 5, 1940, at the age of seventy-five in New Rochelle, New York.

Masculinity as Spectacle

What Cook lacked, among other things, was not simply "proof" but also the endorsements of President Theodore Roosevelt and of organizations like the elite Peary Arctic Club and the National Geographic Society that were powerful purveyors of a nationalist discourse. Part and parcel of that discourse was a gendered concept of heroism associated with the new importance given to the wilderness as a source of national virility and toughness. By the early twentieth century appreciation of the wilderness spread to become a national cult. An increasing number of Americans thought the survival of white masculinity depended upon contact with the wilderness and strenuous physical work.[16] Following the closing of the U.S. frontier announced by Frederick Jackson Turner in 1893, new open spaces such as the Arctic provided a male testing ground where adventure and hardship could still be faced, outside of the weary routine of business and social life at home. Theodore Roosevelt observes in an 1899 men's club speech that confronting the wilderness revitalizes "that vigorous manliness for the lack of which in a nation, as in an individual, the possession of no other qualities can possibly atone."[17] The motivation for Roosevelt's acute concern over the survival of white masculinity was in part a result of the dissolution of the illusionary preindustrial America. Roosevelt feared that the debilitating effect of urban society was fundamentally undermining the willingness and ability of young Anglo-Saxons to pursue active, healthy, and purposeful lives. This concern was also shared by Ernest Thompson Seton, cofounder along with Robert Baden-Powell of the Boy Scout movement at the turn of the century. The purpose of the scouting movement in the

Robert Peary and Theodore Roosevelt shaking hands on the deck of the *S.S. Roosevelt* before Peary's 1908 departure to the Arctic. Roosevelt and Peary were able to establish a mutually authorizing relationship. Roosevelt was one of the major endorsers of Peary's north polar expedition and Peary returned the tribute by naming his ship after him. (Courtesy of the Peary-Macmillan Arctic Museum, Bowdoin College.)

United States, according to Seton in the first *Boy Scouts of America* handbook (1910), was "to combat the system that has turned such a large proportion of our robust, manly, self-reliant boyhood into a lot of flat-chested cigarette smokers, with shaky nerves and doubtful vitality."[18] It was not just too much civilization that was blamed for this incipient state of decline, but a large group of immigrants who were arriving in the country after 1890 that seemed to be diluting the national strain and weakening national traditions. The shifts in immigration patterns as well as women's successful drive for suffrage and increasing influence outside the home presented a potential national threat to the social hierarchy that placed white Euro-American males at the pinnacle.[19]

It is in this context that there is a shift in the meaning of white American masculinity to a Darwinian-based definition in which masculinity as the sporting man / adventurer takes hold.[20] Robert Peary is identified with this new cult of full-blooded manliness by Theodore Roosevelt, who inaugurated this change by coining for this period the revealing phrase "the Strenuous Age." Roosevelt wrote in his preface to Peary's 1910 book:

> Probably few outsiders realize the well-nigh incredible toil and hardship entailed in such an achievement as Peary's. . . . Great physical hardihood and endurance, an iron will and unflinching courage, the power of command, the thirst for adventure, and a keen and far-sighted intelligence—all these must go to the make-up of the successful arctic explorer; and these, and more than these, have gone to the make-up of [Peary] the chief of successful arctic explorers. (*NP*, vii-viii)

Roosevelt praised Peary, and that seems suitable because Peary paid tribute to Roosevelt by naming his ship after him:

> Theodore Roosevelt is to me the most intensely vital man, and the biggest man, America has ever produced. He has that vibrant energy and enthusiasm which is the basis of all real power and accomplishment. When it came to christening the ship by whose aid it was hoped to fight our way toward the most inaccessible spot on earth, the name of *Roosevelt* seemed to be the one and inevitable choice. It held up as ideals before the expedition those very qualities of strength, insistence, persistence, and triumph over obstacles, which have made the twenty-sixth President of the United States so great. (26)

Roosevelt and Peary were able to establish a mutually authorizing relationship because their notions about bodybuilding and nation building were fundamentally similar. In both of their discourses the strenuous life was seen as an antidote to the danger of becoming an "overcivilized man" who in Roosevelt's words "has lost the great fighting, masterful virtues."[21] Roosevelt not only wrote on the strenuous life, but like Robert Peary he lived it, spending considerable time in the 1880s on his ranch in the Dakota territories exulting in the frontiersman's life. Later, when official duties demanded his attention, he still found time for hunting and camping trips in Africa. In 1909 while Peary succeeded at the pole, Roosevelt was in the midst of one of his own African expeditions:

> Camped on the northern foothills of Mt. Kenia, directly under the equator, I received by a native runner the news that he had succeeded, and that thanks to him the discovery of the North Pole was to go on the honor roll of those feats in which we take a peculiar pride because they have been performed by our fellow countrymen. (*NP*, vii)

In the narrative that follows Roosevelt's introduction, the way Peary presents the Arctic is similar to the way Roosevelt presents Africa, as a site on which to recover and stabilize a discourse of virile masculinity that is perceived as having become temporarily decentered and lost.

Peary presents his success in the Arctic as the ultimate test of male self-control. It is a physical challenge in which "real" men can test themselves: "The life is a dog's life, but the work is a man's work" (19). Men who undertake the Arctic challenge are converted by the process into a kernel of energy and a "resourceful" spirit.

Peary constructs himself and the other members of his expeditions as ideal men whose stable identities are exemplified by their successful struggle against the "elements." Peary is distanced and dominating. Yet sometimes in the course of this difficult struggle he is unable to separate himself from objects, other humans, and his own emotions, and his narrative will manifest those anxieties that cut away at his capacity to maintain a stable self-image.

Just before the climax of his narrative, Peary describes his anxieties about the possibility of his failure. He imagines all the possible scenarios, including every possible slip that would prevent him from reaching the goal he has sought for twenty-three years. While his imagination races ahead, he knows that he must constantly check himself. This will be his last attempt, and he reserves all his energy. Yet he is full of anticipation of what is to come:

> Sometimes I would climb to the top of a pinnacle of ice to the north of our camp and strain my eyes into the whiteness which lay beyond, trying to imagine myself already at the pole. We had come so far, and the capricious ice had placed so few obstructions in our path, that now I dared to loose my fancy, to entertain the image which my will had heretofore forbidden to my imagination—the image of ourselves at the goal. (283)

Throughout the narrative Peary emphasizes his ability to remain in control. Yet in this instance, imagining himself at the pole, he momentarily loosens his self-restraint. Although the North Pole, a mathematical point, cannot be perceived except at the site itself and only through a set of observations that require scientific instruments, Peary's literary imagination transforms it into an image visible from afar. From the "top of a pinnacle of ice" he "strains his eyes" and searches through "the whiteness." Peary's narrative begins with the imaginary image of the North Pole and concludes with his so-called faithful record.

However, this tension between Peary's ability to remain in control and to "loose [his] fancy" is a thread that runs through the entire narrative. Peary insists as an older man on his ability to maintain order. Indeed, the issue of his age appears in the first chapter of his narrative:

> I was fifty-three years old, an age beyond which, perhaps, with the exception of Sir John Franklin, no man had ever attempted to prosecute work in the Arctic regions. I was a little past the zenith of my strength, a little lacking, perhaps in the exuberant elasticity and elan of more youthful years, a little past the time when most men begin to leave the strenuous things to the younger generation; but these drawbacks were fully balanced perhaps by a trained and hardened endurance, a perfect knowledge of myself and of how to conserve my strength. (9)

There are advantages to Peary's "perfect knowledge" of himself besides not being easily prone to excitement. The "trained and hardened endurance" he has achieved through years of training are ideal qualities that become the norm by which he judges all the men around him. Indeed, every time he praises another one of his companions, he emphasizes the qualities that take the greatest amount of hard work and discipline to obtain. Close to the climax of his narrative, he even projects his ideals of manhood onto his dogs:

> As I climbed the pressure ridge back of our igloo, I took up another hole in my belt, the third since I left the land—thirty-two days before. Every man and dog of us was as lean and flat-bellied as a board, and as hard. (274)

But although dogs can have disciplined bodies like men, only men are capable of having perfect self-knowledge. An Arctic exploration is the ultimate proof of whether or not they have come close to such an achievement:

> A season in the Arctic is a great test of character. One may know a man better after six months with him beyond the Arctic circle than after a lifetime of acquaintance in cities. There is something—I know not what to call it—in those frozen spaces, that brings a man face to face with himself and with his companions; if he is a man, the man comes out; and if he is a cur, the cur shows as quickly. (19)

According to Peary's logic it is not possible to know in civilization what constitutes masculinity. This belief that a man must face the Arctic wilderness to find out was evidently part of the wider redefinition of masculinity. So much was this the case that it was considered not only desirable but a necessity to accompany Peary to the Arctic circle. In his selection of members of his expedition from a large number of applicants, Peary wanted only a certain kind of man: "A man who could not laugh at a wetting or take as a matter of course a dangerous passage over moving ice, would not be a man for a serious arctic expedition" (108). Robert Bartlett, the captain of the expedition's ship, represented the ideal:

> Blue-eyed, brown-haired, stocky, and steel-muscled Bartlett, whether at the wheel of the *Roosevelt* hammering a passage through the floes, or tramping and stumbling over the ice pack, with the sledges, or smoothing away the troubles of the crew, was always the same—tireless, faithful, enthusiastic, true as the compass. (20)

Peary wanted a "congenial" group for his expedition. The Arctic circle was not a place for a man unable to get along with his fellows.

Josephine Diebitsch-Peary

Despite the tight living quarters during their one-year absence, he notes that there is not much personal friction among his companions: "The principal members of the expedition were men of such character that they were able to exercise an admirable self-restraint that prevented any unpleasant results of consequence" (132). The several voices of his men are silenced in Peary's narrative. There are no discordances, however, as all goes according to plan.

The only white woman in the book is not on the trip. The presence of Mrs. Peary is evoked only at certain moments. She exercises a certain discursive force as part of the hero's persona. She is the nameless "wife" to whom the book is dedicated; she is the cook who made the candy the men opened on Christmas; she is the seamstress of the U.S. flag Peary wears "wrapped about his body" throughout the trek; and she is the addressee of the postcard he writes when he reaches the pole. Peary's marginal references to his wife refer more to Josephine

Diebitsch-Peary's accomplishments within the domestic sphere and hardly suggest that she accompanied Peary on one of his earlier expeditions; nor do they allude to her 1893 published autobiography, *My Arctic Journal: A Year among Ice Fields and Eskimos,* which recounts her trip to the northeast coast of Greenland with her husband before he began his efforts to reach the North Pole.

Now the genre of Arctic exploration narratives is noteworthy in its crucial absence of white women explorers as authors.[22] With few exceptions, even women such as Josephine Diebitsch-Peary seem to have played little more than the role of hyphen, connective, or mere incident in this male genre. Josephine Diebitsch-Peary appears as a mediated and subsidiary person not only when she is framed in certain sites and locations by her husband, but also when she scripts herself into the main narratives. Writing about her experiences she typically presents her public achievements as modest. Though she accompanied her husband on treacherous sledge and boat journeys as well as hunting trips in Greenland, much of her narrative focuses on the time she spent in residence at Redcliffe, her Greenland home in McCormick Bay, while her husband and his men took trips into the interior of Greenland exploring. Doubly removed from the place she had come to explore, she remarks: "I am doing very little besides getting the meals and fixing up odd jobs about the rooms; reading Greely's work is about the extent of my labor."[23] In the following journal entry she hints at her dissatisfaction with the limits imposed by her gender:

> The days are rather unsatisfactory, although I keep busy all day
> sewing, mending, rearranging my room, etc. When I sum up at
> bedtime what I have accomplished, it is very little. Mr. Peary and the
> boys are busily at work on some test sledges. (82)

In passages such as this one Josephine Diebitsch-Peary shows how conforming to acceptable female behavior excluded her from participating in some of the expedition's varied chores and activities. Her dissatisfaction emphasizes the conflict between maintaining her respectability as a woman, which meant not exposing herself engaged in work considered unfeminine, and her desire to be an explorer. In her writings the unmapped spaces of the Arctic are seen as officially the realm of and for men; for her to enter the space outside of Redcliffe without being accompanied by her husband entailed unforeseen risks. Exposing oneself in public was not only considered a liability for women in the Arctic; it was equally dangerous at home in the world of geographical societies, clubs, and publishing houses that was also defined as exclusive to men. Since respectable femininity was understood within an arrangement of familial domesticity, Josephine Diebitsch-Peary's inclusion was dependent on her husband's authorization. In his prefatory note to her Arctic journal, Robert Peary associates his wife's natural gender and class position with the narrative's style and meaning. It is a "plain and simple narrative" written by "a refined woman" who "shrank from publicity" and only "reluctantly yielded to the idea that her experiences might be of interest to others besides her immediate friends" (3). Women can no more engage in writing than in exploration without male mediation and authentication, and Josephine Diebitsch-Peary offers little other evidence in her journal to counter this image, as her text is also structured by an opposition between home, the inside domain of refinement and constrained personality, and the outside, the space of freedom where she has only limited access. Her awareness of femininity's class-specific forms may have contributed to her reluctance in positing a different kind of self-presentation, the kind of image that was also more safely displayed by her husband, halfway through his preface to her book:

> I rarely, if ever, take up the thread of our Arctic experiences without referring to two pictures: one is the first night that we spent on the Greenland shore after the departure of the "Kite," when in a little tent on the rocks—a tent which the furious wind threatened every moment to carry away bodily—she watched by my side as I lay a helpless cripple with a broken leg. . . . Long afterward she told me that every unwonted sound of the wind set her heart beating with the thoughts of some hungry bear roaming along the shore and attracted by the unusual sight of the tent; yet she never gave a sign at the time of her fears, lest it should disturb me.
>
> The other picture is that of a scene perhaps a month or two later, when—myself still a cripple, but not entirely helpless—this same woman sat for an hour beside me in the stern of a boat, calmly reloading our empty firearms while a herd of infuriated walrus about us thrust their savage heads with gleaming tusks and bloodshot eyes out of the water close to the muzzles of our rifles. . . . I may perhaps

be pardoned for saying that I never think of these two experiences without a thrill of pride and admiration for her pluck. (4-5)

In this passage Peary still dominates the narrative; it is only as part of his persona that his wife gains certain unique attributes such as "pluck." Indeed, Josephine Diebitsch-Peary's existence is limited to that of a devoted wife who blossoms only when her husband is in need. Robert Peary's claim that his wife was "special" in this context enables her both to excel as his wife as well as to fit conventional parameters of femininity. According to Dea Birkett's study in *Spinsters Abroad: Victorian Lady Explorers*, such male claims of women's uniqueness were also aimed at "softening the threat" of "New Women" who were taking part in great numbers in exploration from the late nineteenth century onward. Birkett contends that "stressing their uniqueness was a way to establish them as exceptions rather than representatives of a growing trend."[24]

The stress given to Josephine Diebitsch-Peary's "special" qualities is reiterated by her publishers, who heroicize her as the first white woman and "civilized being" seen by some Eskimos in the Arctic region:

> In the following pages Mrs. Peary recounts her experiences of a full twelve months spent on the shores of McCormick Bay, midway between the Arctic Circle and the North Pole. The Eskimos with whom she came in contact belong to a little tribe of about three hundred and fifty individuals, completely isolated from the rest of the world. They are separated by hundreds of miles from their nearest neighbors, with whom they have no intercourse whatever. These people had never seen a white woman, and some of them had never beheld a civilized being. The opportunities which Mrs. Peary had of observing their manners and mode of life have enabled her to make a valuable contribution to ethnological learning. (2)

There is a peculiar dynamic produced by how she is framed by her publishers, by her husband, and by herself in terms of her racial and sexual identity. Though the publishers' introductory note sets up the expectation that her gender would enable her to portray the Eskimo society with a specially keen eye, she, ironically, is the least sympathetic portrayer of nonwhite people. Indeed, her diary is noteworthy for the callousness she exercises toward her Eskimo employees, which rivals that of the most brutal of male explorers. Like her husband, she neither displays nor argues for any of the cultural relativism present in other writings of the period and continually employs evaluative terms in her repeated references to Eskimos as "huskies," "pickaninnies," "semi-savages," and "monkeys." However, her antipathy toward Eskimo women was even more excessive than her husband's, as when she likens an Eskimo seamstress to "a new broom" that she hopes "wears well" (*MAJ*, 87). This aversion could be understood within an arrangement of familial domesticity set up by her husband in which he cast her in rivalry with Eskimo women (particularly his mistress) and thus set her up to compete. Given the threat Eskimo women posed in terms of her own marriage, it would seem that the very condition of her own inclusion, with some dignity, in the mainstream narrative of male exploration and female domesticity involves her writing about other women in subordinate positions much in the way that her husband's self-presentation involved inscribing her.

If Josephine Diebitsch-Peary was presented as a constrained and modest personality, her husband posits a different self-presentation. Peary's own boundlessness is embodied in the monumental scale of his project, which seemed to be part of its appeal. When one of the major contributors to the expedition died and Peary was uncertain whether or not he would get the funding he needed, he restored his own confidence with the belief that "the project was something too big to die; and it never, in the great scheme of things, would be allowed to fall through" (*NP*, 15). *Big* is a key word for Peary in defining the North Pole project. It was also used by the project's financiers. Zenas Crane, a Massachusetts paper manufacturer and member of the Peary Arctic Club, believed that "Peary's project was one which should have the support of everyone who cared for big things and for the prestige of the country" (16-17).

There was an equivalence between the bombastic rhetoric of Peary and Crane and the expedition's exaggerated scale. Indeed, there were no small unfilled corners aboard Peary's ship. Its extensive inventory included: a "fairly complete arctic library," "a large assortment of novels and magazines," "a pianola and an extensive collection of two hundred pieces of music." Peary's taste in music verged on the grand and monumental:

The strains of "Faust" rolled out over the Arctic Ocean more often than any other. Marches and songs were also popular, with the Blue Danube waltz; and sometimes, when the spirits of my party were at rather a low ebb, we had ragtime pieces. (31)

The image Peary gives of his expedition's ship is that of a kind of self-sufficient enclosure. He describes his cabin as a place of cherished seclusion that not only offers many of the comforts of home but very closely resembles it:

> I have a special affection for my little cabin on the *Roosevelt*. Its size and the comfort of the bathroom adjoining were the only luxuries which I allowed myself. . . . It has a wide built-in bunk, an ordinary writing desk, several book units, a wicker chair, an office chair, and a chest of drawers, these latter items of furniture being Mrs. Peary's contributions to my comfort. Hanging over the pianola was a photograph of Mr. Jesup, and on the side wall was one of President Roosevelt, autographed. Then there were the flags, the silk one made by Mrs. Peary, which I had carried for years, the flag of my college fraternity, Delta Kappa Epsilon, the flag of the Navy League, and the peace flag of the Daughters of the American Revolution. There was also a photograph of our home on Eagle Island, and a fragment pillow made by my daughter Marie from the pine needles of that island. (30-31)

If the interior of Peary's cabin on the ship resembles the intimate and cluttered spaces of an early twentieth-century house in the United States, the materials of its exterior are identified with the public spaces of U.S. industry:

> The *Roosevelt* was built of American timber in an American shipyard, engined by an American firm with American metal, and constructed on American designs. (19)

The image of Peary's ship is that of a self-sufficient U.S. totality. Peary never leaves home in the sense that he continues to inhabit a simulacrum of home while he is away. Any reality he encounters that is incompatible with his own he literally transforms to a known and familiar space by filling it with his own personal furnishings. An example of this tendency of Peary's is his impulse to plant his fraternity flag at the North Pole.

Peary explains in his narrative that his expedition generated a great deal of public interest in the United States. Despite most of the project's funding coming from a group of U.S. millionaires, there was also a populist edge to the project. Peary received small donations ranging from $100 to $1 as well as letters of advice from private citizens:

> A small flood of "crank" letters poured in from all over the country. There was an incredibly large number of persons who were simply oozing with inventions and schemes, the adoption of which would absolutely ensure the discovery of the Pole. . . . Flying machines occupied a high place on the list. Motor cars, guaranteed to run over any kind of ice, came next.
>
> Another chap proposed that a central soup station be installed . . . and that a series of hose lines be run thence over the ice so that the outlying parties struggling over the ice to the Pole could be warmed and invigorated with hot soup from the central station.
>
> Perhaps the gem of the whole collection was furnished by an inventor who desired me to play the part of the human cannon-ball. . . . This was surely a man of one idea. He was so intent on getting me shot to the Pole that he seemed to be utterly careless of what happened to me in the process of landing there or of how I should get back. (18)

Although Peary emphasizes the difference between his expedition and the "crank letters," actually the two have much more in common than he might like to admit. One of the fantastic features of Peary's expedition is his conception of men and dogs as technology:

> Man and the Eskimo dog are the only two machines capable of such adjustments as to meet the wide demands and contingencies of Arctic travel. Airships, motor cars, trained polar bears, etc., are all premature, except as a means of attracting public attention. (5)

Peary evaluates trained polar bears, cars, and airplanes equally. He considers each a premature form of technology for this period of Arctic travel. For Peary, the most effective "instruments" for Arctic work were the Eskimos.[25] Thus he hired an entire Eskimo village to fulfill the needs of his project:

> I have often been asked: Of what use are Eskimos to the world? They are too far removed to be of value for commercial enterprises and, furthermore, they lack ambition. They have no literature nor, properly speaking, any art. They value life only as does a fox, or a bear, purely by instinct. But let us not forget that these people, trustworthy and hardy, will yet prove their value to mankind. With their help, the world shall discover the Pole. (NP, 43)

What was peculiar to Peary's adoption of the Eskimos as a work force for his expedition was the emphasis in his writing on how he was responsible for their mental and physical evolution. As benign master, Peary trains his "children" in skills he deems useful for his expedition, from hunting and sledging to sewing. In so doing he discursively elevates them from persons who live like animals without language, culture, commerce, or art into citizens of the world who will "yet prove their value to mankind." He then pays them with cheap trade goods brought from the United States, while living in large part off the land and off the fruits of the Eskimos' hunting endeavors. In the name of "progress," what begins as an association of companions very quickly becomes one of creditor and debtor, and soon becomes that of the colonizer and the colonized:

> Since 1891 I had been living and working with these people, gaining their absolute confidence, making them my debtors for things given them, earning their gratitude. For 18 years I had been training them in my methods. . . . I have been studying the Eskimos and no more effective instruments for arctic work could be imagined than these plump, bronze-skinned, keen-eyed and black-maned children of nature. (43-44)

Peary's purpose is to convert his "children of nature" into what he termed "technology" that fuels his "traveling machine." Peary writes of his expedition as something of a model of uniformed mass production, a perfectly efficient factory that standardizes the making of workers. Through this system Peary fixes subjects and systems of difference. He refers to the indigenous members of his expedition either as "cogs," "hyperborean aborigines," or "savages" (5-6). He refers to Matthew Henson as his "negro bodyservant" (272). Often he mentions the Eskimo dogs in relation to their function of providing the "tractive force" for the sleds (8). Peary strives to make these hierarchical orders appear natural, yet he does not try to conceal the inequalities of colonial power. Rather, he reveals it to be a part of the workings of his expedition's technology.

Peary rewrites the Inuit in the idiom of scientific management in order to establish absolute power hierarchies in which all others— Eskimos and blacks—are subordinate to him. Peary's relations with the Inuits provide a startling contrast to Cook's, who admits to losing the absolute forms of power that Peary exercised. Cook writes about how his struggle against death is averted through the bonds of friendship he established with two Inuit men. On Cook's return from the pole, he and his two Inuit companions get lost and are all forced to spend the Arctic night in a cave together before returning to their base during the following Arctic summer. Cook writes that his survival depended on merging his identity with that of his native companions:

> We were now a family unit and by the harmony within that union our world must be determined. We were co-defendants in a self-determination where interdependent manhood of a high order was important. (*RP*, 103)

Unlike Peary, who discursively prevents himself from becoming too vulnerable to the Inuits by likening them to technology, Cook's dependence on his Inuit companions enables him to enjoy reciprocal relations with them. Cook emphasizes "the mutual confidence and trust established between them" (280) and recounts how they freely risked their lives for his as he did for theirs. He goes native in order to survive with them and emphasizes how their companionship prevented him from becoming lonely and depressed. By the end of his stay, he writes:

> Brotherhood is a far-reaching emotion, and to a brotherly interdependence more than to any other social trait must be ascribed our eventual success. Here we have dealt with primitive life of the cave-man days. My two companions were but a generation or two above the Stone Age. They rose to an emergency requiring a high order of intelligence. I reverted and reacted to the basic urgency of the primitive. Together we suffered and worked as brothers to feed and shelter and protect each other. (314)

Cook constructs a utopian society out of this interracial friendship, while at the same time admitting that this insight was brought on by his extraordinary circumstances. Always under the threat of death, none of them could afford to disagree, with starvation and cannibalism always being possibilities. Cook maintains his generally evolutionist way of thinking to explain his experience of reverting to a primitive stage as well as the Inuit's rapid evolution to a high order of intelligence. Literally becoming an Eskimo is part of the Arctic's fascination for him. Yet it is only a temporary cultural state for Cook, who believed that race was only permanently transmitted genetically.

Once he returned to the United States he would be able to shed his Eskimo skin.

At the North Pole: The Coitus of Discovery

If the discovery of the North Pole had various meanings for Cook, which included the gaining of self-knowledge through overcoming obstacles of racial difference, Peary was more concerned with fulfilling recognizable norms of heroism and manliness. His singular goal was clearly to identify and make known what was previously understood as an indefinable scene beyond the realm of reality:

> Through all the seasons of disappointment and defeat I had never ceased to believe that the great white mystery of the North must eventually succumb to the insistence of human experience and will. (*NP*, 41)

The key to Peary's success is in denying as far as possible the reality of his Arctic surroundings and "faithfully" carrying out instead the details of his plan he has worked out in advance. Although he insists on his ability to remain objective and to behave rationally, when he arrives at the pole he has difficulty maintaining self-mastery. Some hours after his arrival at the pole, Peary writes the following in his journal; it was first published in the *National Geographic* in October 1909:

> The pole at last! The prize of three centuries. My dream and goal for twenty years! Mine at last! I cannot bring myself to realize it. It all seems so simple and commonplace. As Bartlett said when turning back, when speaking of his being in these exclusive regions which no mortal has ever penetrated before, "It's just like every day."
>
> Of course I had my sensations that made sleep impossible for hours, despite my utter fatigue—the sensations of a lifetime; but I have no room for them here. The first thirty hours at the Pole were spent in taking observations; in going some ten miles beyond our camp, and some eight miles to the right of it; in taking photographs, planting my flags, depositing my records, studying the horizon with my telescope for possible land, and searching for a practicable place to make a sounding. . . .
>
> We had reached the goal, but the return was still before us. It was essential that we reach the land before the next spring tide, and we must strain every nerve to do this.[26]

Frederick Cook wrote the following account of his polar experiences, which he, too, published in *National Geographic* in 1909:

Slowly but surely we neared the turning point. Good astronomical observations were daily procured to fix the advancing stages.

The ice steadily improved, but still there was a depressing monotony of scene, and life had no pleasures, no spiritual recreation, nothing to relieve the steady physical drag of chronic fatigue.

But there came an end to this as to all things. On April 21 the first corrected altitude of the sun gave 89 deg. 59 min. 46 sec.

The Pole, therefore, was in sight.

We advanced the fourteen seconds, made supplementary observations and prepared to stay long enough to permit a double round of observations.

Etukishook and Ahwelab were told that we had reached the "Neig Nail" and they sought to celebrate by an advance of savage joys.

At last we had pierced the boreal center and the flag had been raised to the coveted breezes of the North Pole.

The day was April 21, 1908. The sun indicated local noon, but time was a negative problem, for here all meridians meet.

With a step it was possible to go from one part of the globe to the opposite side.

From the hour of midnight to that of midday the latitude was 90, the temperature 38 and the barometer 29.83.

North, east and west had vanished. It was south in every direction, but the compass pointing to the magnetic pole was as useful as ever.

Though overjoyed with the success of the conquest, our spirits began to descend on the following day. After all the observations had been taken with a careful study of the local conditions a sense of intense loneliness came with the further scrutiny of the horizon.

What a cheerless spot to have aroused the ambition of man for so many ages!

An endless field of purple snows. No life. No land. No spot to relieve the monotony of frost. We were the only pulsating creatures in a dead world of ice.

We turned our backs to the pole on April 23 and began the long return march.[27]

In both Peary's and Cook's accounts of their arrival at the North Pole, there is the realization that they have risked their lives to act out an illusory spectacle. This is more than just an expression of disappointment or surprise in finding literally nothing visibly different about this privileged spot. Once found, the anticipatory value of its discovery is lost. After its discovery, for Cook the pole was merely "a dead world of ice" that he preferred to turn his back on. Peary, on his arrival at the pole, experienced his discovery as "simple and commonplace." "It's just like every day."

Both Peary's and Cook's descriptions of their experience at the pole emphasize the sensations of the technological extension of their human body over the body itself. The props of discovery and conquest—the compass, the telescope, the flag, and the camera—take on a hyperreal significance in each of their accounts. The compass is the one thing that is "as useful as ever" for Cook. In his description it becomes the only indication of life, as his group is just barely alive, "pulsating creatures in a dead world of ice." Cook's own identification with his compass enables him to experience a sense of euphoria in which he imagines himself for a brief moment outside his own experience of extreme sensory deprivation. "North, east and west had vanished. It was south in every direction." "With a step it was possible to go from one part of the globe to the opposite side." Peary's euphoria instead is about his ability to transcend his dependency on his instruments. He uses his instruments but triumphs over them because he can choose his experience. He uses his instruments selectively to achieve the control he wants. But only to a point. For Peary and Cook the North Pole is perceivable only through scientific instruments. Nothing can be observed. The redundancy of the eye with a sighting of the pole can only be technological, not personal. Hence in Cook's account the phrase "scientific observation" refers to calculations, the very opposite of observations. "On April 21 the first corrected altitude of the sun gave 89 deg. 59 min. 46 sec. The pole, therefore, was in sight. We advanced the fourteen seconds, made supplementary observations and prepared to stay long enough to permit a double round of observations" (894).

By personalizing the impersonal ("Mine at last"), Peary desperately tries to hold on to his status as a hero and thus to claim something that he cannot see or feel. His image of "his being in these exclusive regions which no mortal has ever penetrated before" seems incongruous with his actual activity of "taking photographs, planting my flags, ... studying the horizon with my telescope for possible land, and searching for a place to make a sounding." No wonder his "dream and goal for twenty years" all seemed "so simple and commonplace" once he reached the site itself.

In Cook's account there is the difficulty of finding a common denominator in which to reconcile the neutral and impersonal quality of his surroundings with a personal experience of conquest. "The depressing monotony of scene" (894) and its lack of any spiritual pleasure only expresses for him "his steady physical drag of chronic fatigue" (894). Rather than offering any form of relief, a "further scrutiny of the horizon" brings on a "sense of intense loneliness" (895). In his 1913 autobiography entitled *My Attainment of the Pole*, Cook speaks of his own disillusionment:

> After spending two days at the Pole . . . the glamour wore away . . . I could get no sensation of novelty . . . hungry, mentally and physically exhausted, a sense of the utter uselessness of this thing, of the empty reward of my endurance, followed my exhilaration. . . . During these last hours I asked myself why this place had so aroused an enthusiasm long-lasting through self-sacrificing years; why, for so many centuries, men had sought this elusive spot? What a futile thing, I thought, to die for![28]

Cook realizes his part in what he now calls a "travesty, an ironic satire, a vainglorious human aspiration and endeavor." From his earlier image of the pole, which was one of splendor and plentitude, this new image is of a "silver-shining goal of death."

Unlike Peary and Cook, Matthew Henson does not write about a euphoric relation to his instruments in his 1913 autobiographical account, *A Negro Explorer at the North Pole*. As he is denied access to the tools of science, Henson, Peary's body servant, does not know when he has reached the pole. He has to wait until Peary tells him. Peary writes that he relies on Henson's "intuitive" sense of gauging distances for most of the trip, yet when they reach the pole, Henson is reliant on Peary.

The instruments take on a subject position in Henson's narrative. Indeed, they are treated as an extension of Peary himself, and as such are endowed with more value than Henson's own life. Because Henson is denied an official share in Peary's discovery of the pole until afterward, when there is a collective flag-raising ceremony for the nonwhite members of the polar party, he reserves his euphoria for later. Henson celebrates U.S. democracy from the position of a servant who cannot share in the same festivities as his master can:

> The Commander gave the word. "We will plant the stars

Matthew Henson

and stripes—AT THE NORTH POLE and it was done; on the peak of a huge paleocrystic floeberg the glorious banner was unfurled to the breeze, and as it snapped and crackled with the wind, I felt a savage joy and exultation. Another world's accomplishment was done and finished, and in the past, from the beginning of history, wherever the world's work was done by a white man, he had been accompanied by a colored man. From the building of the pyramids and the journey to the Cross, to the discovery of the North Pole, the Negro had been the faithful and constant companion of the Caucasian, and I felt all that it was possible for me to feel, that it was I, a lowly member of my race, who had been chosen by fate to represent it, at this, almost the last of the world's great WORK.[29]

The official public discourse available to Henson allows him to participate in the discovery of the North Pole, but not to claim an individual identity in relation to his success. Thus, in his account of his discovery of the North Pole, he describes a collective rather than an individual experience. He reveals a pride in his race, not in his sense of self. By positioning his racial self within the same historical perspective as that of his white master, Henson's message at the North Pole is not one of difference but of value. He accepts his color as a sign of a racial essence but does not accept that the cultural capacities of the African American are inferior to those of the Caucasian. Instead, he aligns himself with other African Americans who like himself have proved their physical and intellectual capacities by participating in what white men consider to be "great" work. Now the "greatness" of this work was of course that of Western colonial expansion, which, although white, made claims to inclusive universality.

National Geographic Magazine and Robert Peary: Refurbishing the Myth

Of all the men who trekked across a barren wasteland of crashing ice floes to obtain the North Pole, Robert Peary alone became a national hero. This was due to his validation by the National Geographic Society in 1909. I have already indicated that his discovery continues to be contested. In 1988 the fact that Peary's purported discovery was disproved didn't prevent Peary from being honored in *National Geographic*'s centennial issue. Matthew Henson, the black explorer who accompanied Peary, also receives the legitimacy that he lacked in

Robert Peary took this photograph of Matthew Henson and the four Inuits—
Ooqueah, Oohtah, Egingwah, and Seegloo—at the so-called North Pole. The
way the individual identities of all these men of color are subordinated to
that of the American flag is in line with existing Euro-American photographic
conventions of the period, which tended to represent distant and remote
places through photographs of local "native inhabitants" whose function was
primarily as decorative objects, signs of the exotic.

1909, but ironically his recognition comes now that he is dead and when it is established that Peary never made it to the pole.[30] What is surprising is how British explorer and *National Geographic* writer Wally Herbert turns this new twist in events to Peary's advantage. Even as Herbert contests the accuracy of Peary's claims, he is able to avoid stigmatizing Peary as simply incompetent by rendering his folly forgivable or even praiseworthy. By rhetorically framing Peary as a suffering and misunderstood hero, Herbert preserves Peary's integrity. He does this by quoting a previously unpublished letter from Peary's wife. We learn that it was not Peary's "sixteen years of research in the Arctic regions" that accounted for the "breaking down of his iron constitution." Rather, the hardships that he suffered from the most were inflicted on him by his own government:

> The personal grilling which he was obliged to undergo at the hands
> of Congress . . . although it resulted in his complete vindication . . .
> did more toward the breaking down of his iron constitution than
> anything experienced in his explorations.[31]

Even for Herbert, Peary's pretenses of sovereignty, supremacy, and honor needed challenging. Honor followed, as it were, the colonizing path of the empire builder. In Herbert's words:

> Peary was not being driven by the rational mind but by the
> conviction that the pole was his and that he had the divine right to
> discover it and return to proclaim his achievement. (413)

Oddly enough, this perception does not lead Herbert to a critique of the validity of Peary's entitlement but to an appreciation of the emotional costs Peary had to undergo to fulfill the imperial norm. According to Herbert, it did not matter whether or not Peary reached the pole; Peary was a visionary of empire and should have been above all criticism:

> As to whether or not Peary reached the North Pole, the answer, by
> the nature of the subject elements within it, can never be anything
> more than a probability. Regardless of the answer, from the higher
> ground of history Peary stands out as a pioneer who contributed to
> mankind. Impelled by the energy of his obsession, conquering with
> his exceptional courage man's fear of the unknown, he extended the
> bounds of human endeavor. Thus was his mission a success. (413)

It is Peary the pioneer, the hero who "extended the bounds of human endeavor," who enables Herbert to retell the story of Peary's last expedition as a positive measure of his creativity and originality. By historical hindsight, Peary was a great man who "contributed to mankind" even though Herbert shows that he failed from a scientific perspective. The question of failure haunts Peary's expedition, though in ways different from the discourse that frames the catastrophic attempt of the British naval officer Scott on his return from the South Pole. It is significant that Herbert, a British explorer and writer, attempts to explain Peary's heroism along the lines of a British national tradition. However, this rewriting is unacceptable in the tradition of *National Geographic* heroism.

Herbert's articulation of the Peary myth is based on a British notion of inner worth rather than on the U.S. discourse of methodical science and technology. Herbert quotes Theodore Roosevelt, who touted Peary as an antidote "to the softening tendencies of our time" (401), in order to suggest that the current image of the Peary who lost most of his toes in the Arctic is more human than Roosevelt's idealized conception of him. This enables Herbert to readjust the Roosevelt myth of Peary down to human scale by shifting the emphasis from technological prowess to strength of character.

As I suggested earlier, Herbert's report tried to legitimize Peary's failure, but his conclusions did not fit within the *Geographic* tradition in which scientific ability is the foremost sign of male power and achievement. Thus, Herbert's gesture of recuperation was later perceived by the *Geographic* as a threat that demanded containment. To preempt any further critical analysis of Peary, the *Geographic* later commissioned the Foundation for the Promotion of the Art of Navigation to reinvestigate Peary's findings. This time the research worked out in the *Geographic* 's favor by proving that Peary made it to the pole after all.

A faded black-and-white photograph taken during Peary's 1909 expedition is used as *documentary* evidence, telling it like it is. The shadows in the image are used as clues to find the sun's elevation, which was compared with the declination of the sun for the date and the time indicated in the *Nautical Almanac*. The altitude of the sun measured from the photograph was used to confirm Peary's location. Such an analysis based on an eighty-year-old photograph involves just as much artifice as does any other mode of visual representation; the "unimpeachable findings" of the Navigation Foundation appear no more convincing or truthful than any other facts in this case offered by the society in its earliest days. Thomas Davies's account of the report in the *National Geographic* demonstrates how Peary's original photographs at the pole are used to embody a particular kind of truth and authenticity:

> Our final and most conclusive examination was of the photographs taken by Peary near Camp Jesup. Since an inadequate attempt by merchant captain Thomas Hall in *Did Peary Reach the Pole?* (1917), there seems to have been no real analysis of Peary's photographs; accordingly our efforts represent new evidence. Techniques of photographic analysis that were pioneered during World War II developed into a fine craft during the Cold War years of satellite observation. One technique, called photogrammetric rectification, can produce the angle of the elevations of the sun from the shadows in pictures.[32]

Applying the latest in cold war modern photographic technology to confirm the validity of Peary's word, Davies's article again uses an ideology of positivism to determine justly that Peary is the rightful winner.

2

National Geographic Society and Magazine: Technologies of Nationalism, Race, and Gender

*In the modern world, everyone can, should, will "have" a
nationality, as he or she "has" a gender.*

—Benedict Anderson, *Imagined Communities*

Theorists of nationalism such as Benedict Anderson argue that the
spread of print culture during the early 1800s in Europe was central
to constituting new national identities.[1] As Anderson points out, the
modernity of nationalism can be seen in the peculiar way that novels,
newspapers, and magazines provided a common language that enabled people to form collective identities. Though Anderson's theory
of nationalism is helpful in connecting the narrative fascination of the
popular media to the constitution of national imaginations, his ideas
do not account for the way that this process is inflected by distinct
gender representations that are peculiar to a national tradition in the
United States. Thus, while Anderson points to gender in the quotation that introduces this chapter, what is missing from his theory, and
indeed from his study, is an understanding of the broad process of gender exclusion and racial discrimination that occurs within the domains
of discourse and institutional practices that sanction nationalism.[2]

In considering how particular constructions of gender, race, and
class are articulated with an ideology of nationalism in U.S. mass media, my focus falls on the beginnings of *National Geographic*, an influential magazine and society in the United States that appropriated
nationalism and popularized identity as essentially a white masculine
one. This study suggests that, despite its commercial nature, the *National Geographic* was able to occupy the discursive space that nor-
mally belonged to governmental institutions.

The *Geographic*'s past discourse on Peary's polar exploration was symptomatic of the way the *National Geographic* generally used a discourse of nationalism, empire, and white male heroism to justify its own identity and to install itself as an authoritative medium of cultural communication at the turn of the century. An examination of the *Geographic*'s past is relevant to the society's self-representation in the present. In chapters 1 and 3, emphasis has been placed on how representations of early *Geographic* explorers such as Peary have become increasingly popular in recent years, from the September 1988 centennial issue of the *National Geographic* magazine to the 1988 *National Geographic* video special *The Explorers: A Century of Discovery*. This popularity marks more than an acceptance of early explorations and the deeds of "great" *Geographic* explorers. Rather, representations of this sort have been successfully employed as vehicles to articulate a renewed sense of tradition and national belonging that is defined in a manner that is equally excluding and, more significantly, equally damaging to women and people of color. An examination of the society's origins will establish a context for understanding the *Geographic*'s more recent practices of exclusion.[3]

The Construction of the National Geographic as an Authorized Purveyor of Knowledge

The National Geographic's first magazine was published in October 1888. The earliest volumes were devoted primarily to scientific professionals. One reviewer criticized it for being "dreadfully scientific . . . suitable for diffusing geographic knowledge among those who already had it and scaring off the rest."[4] In 1899, ten years after the first issue of the *National Geographic* appeared, the magazine was facing premature bankruptcy. To save the *National Geographic*, Alexander Graham Bell, the inventor of the telephone and second president of the National Geographic Society, came up with a plan to attract a wider audience:

> Why not popularize the science of geography and take it into the homes of the people? Why not transform the Society's magazine from one of cold geographic fact, expressed in hieroglyphic terms which the layman could not understand, into a vehicle for carrying the living, breathing, human-interest truth about this great world of ours

to the people? Would not that be the greatest agency of all for the diffusion of geographic knowledge?[5]

The *National Geographic* was quite open about its new approach and frequently published accounts such as the one cited above linking its growth and prosperity to its plan to popularize science. In this way it distinguished itself from professional scientific journals, which Bell criticized as "cold" and incomprehensible. Professional science served as the necessary foil, the essential negative opposition, that by contrast gave substance to the superiority of the *Geographic*'s new populist approach, which identified itself with U.S. democratic ideals. So successful was this tactic that professional scientific organizations, in response to the popularity of organizations like the National Geographic Society, were often put on the defensive to differentiate themselves from their amateur counterparts. Thus, according to Preston James, a graduate student in geography in the early 1920s:

> For many years after 1897, people who thought of themselves as geographical scholars, not people with a diffuse interest in exploration and adventure, became more and more scornful of the NGS magazine. . . . The general public, on hearing that one was a geographer, would usually reply, "Oh, do you work for the NGS?" The only possible attitude for the young geographers of the 20's and 30's was scorn for all this. So Gilbert Grosvenor was never invited to sit at the speakers table at the American Geographical Society banquets, or even to attend meetings. ("NGS," 527)

Although science had become a profession by the early part of the twentieth century, the new scientists had no recognized authority outside of the public institutions where they worked. In a democracy that lacked a sense of hierarchy, a social structure, and a system of deference associated with scientific societies of Western Europe, these new professionals working in universities and government found it difficult to gain respect.[6] The *National Geographic* magazine, on the other hand, began to prosper and obtain a measure of public recognition by incorporating popular perceptions and resentments toward these new professionals that it then reshaped and reaffiliated in the course of its appeal to legitimize itself as a respectable alternative. Still, if the *Geographic* from its inception tried to distinguish itself from the discourse of professional science, neither did it want to become associated with the discourse of a literary enterprise, the stuff of lending libraries and fictional bestsellers, which was coded as feminine activity. It is significant that *Geographic* editors stressed the absence of fiction in its pages in order to acquire a prestige that was otherwise denied to discourses of mass culture.[7] By identifying the magazine with the new technology of photography and the areas of science and industry, the *Geographic* maintained its distance from literature—primarily the realm of the subjective and the emotional—and established itself as the domain of the authentic and the genuine, the privileged realm of male activities and truth.

Truth and Technology = Seeing Is Believing

The *National Geographic* benefited immensely from taking advantage of new technological advances. The Kodak No. 1, the first portable roll-film camera, the dry plate, and the halftone screen for photoengraving had all been developed in the 1880s, making photography for the first time a practicable means of illustration. The large number of improvements in photographic technology brought about cheaper and more convenient methods of production. The *National Geographic* magazine was one of the first U.S. publications to seize on these innovations and utilize photographs. The first photographs appeared in *National Geographic* in 1896 when a halftone frontispiece was introduced. Over the next few years the use of photographs grew steadily, and they improved gradually in quality. By 1908 the magazine devoted half of its eighty pages to photographs and illustrations and by 1910 displayed the first color pictures. By 1924 half the issues had color sections, and by 1928 all of them did.

The rapid success of the *National Geographic* under Grosvenor's editorial leadership depended on the magazine's use of photography and the authority that began to accrue to photographic representations as reality itself. There was the belief that visualizing a culture or place became synonymous for actually being there. With the advent of photography, participating in world events as they happened was considered possible. Knowledge of all non-Western cultures represented by the *Geographic* could be obtained simply through photographic representations of the world. The absence of scientific jargon or of analytical data that were difficult to follow made the magazine intelligible to the average reader. Editorial policy emphasized having "accurate eyewitness, firsthand accounts" expressed in "writing that sought to make pictures in the reader's mind." Bell noted that "judging by myself, the pictures are the first thing looked at."[8] According to letters sent in, readers wanted immediate experience of the world, not the geographical lessons professionals sought to provide. And Grosvenor felt "that we should give our members what they wanted, not what some specialist thought they should have" (34). This policy enabled those who possessed expertise and those who did not to participate equally in the *Geographic*'s enterprise.

Photographic technology offered an alternative to lived reality, enabling the *National Geographic* readership to become accomplished travelers through subscribing to the magazine. Without discomfort or expense these readers might be able to claim a proprietary interest in the geography of the world through their consumption of each monthly issue. Maps that accompanied every article also had an important function in helping make a distant and unfamiliar world legible and understandable to the reader. By being able to situate the world through mapping, each *National Geographic* subscriber would be able to participate in geographical problems that would otherwise remain only the privileged realm of experts or of an upper-class group of world travelers.

New technologies such as photography were thought to break down orders of social difference and thus appeared by their very nature to be more democratic than the hierarchical discourse of professional scientists. Indeed, by popularizing the subject of geography the *Geographic* was able to infuse new energy into this field, according to Phillip Pauley, a historian of science, who points out how the scientific status of the field's central activity, exploration, was declining:

> The successful penetration into "darkest Africa" had left the polar regions as the only large empty spaces on the world map. The economic, political or scientific value of such exploration was considered dubious by a group of eminent scientists who were polled in 1894. ("NGS," 518)

In contrast to professional scientists who were interested in the potential of geography as a militarily useful study, the *Geographic*'s scientific project explored other spaces besides those that had an explicit political value for a colonialist project. The poles evoked particular interest because they enabled the *Geographic* to portray exploration as an aesthetic, disinterested activity completely autonomous from any commercial or colonialist practice, and thus to sustain a noncontroversial image of itself. What was particular to polar exploration discourse was a certain dependency on technology, not only to find with instruments the mathematical spot of the pole itself and to record the event of its discovery, but to actually get there. Like the *Geographic* itself that substituted representations for actual travel, the North Pole was a site in which early twentieth-century technologies and representations produced by these technologies (navigational charts and calculations that would measure longitude and latitude as well as check for compass variations along the route) were necessary mediators.

It is important to recall that Peary's discourse upsets conventional notions of what constitutes "technology" by including Eskimo men and women as well as dogs in its definition. Peary used native peoples and animals to exercise his control in a region and climate that he was unfamiliar with. Thus what he refers to as his "traveling machine" actually consisted of technically advanced Western ships and navigational equipment as well as Eskimo peoples and dogs, who are included on the basis of the function they served. All were considered equally essential to bolster Peary's own ends in expanding the range of what was previously considered humanly possible.

Democracy and Science

Grosvenor and Bell's interest in establishing a society that would take the science of geography into Americans' homes turned on an exemplary marriage of U.S. democracy and U.S. technology. Using the magazine as a tool to attract members, Bell and Grosvenor's project was to build up a great national scientific society comprised of large masses of people. By blurring the boundaries between membership in an elite society and subscriptions to a popular magazine, the National Geographic Society was meant to be more than a magazine, as there was status connected to being a member of a society that sponsored explorations such as Peary's expedition to the North Pole. Grosvenor explained in a letter to the journalist Ida Tarbell in 1900:

A combination of membership and magazine will be a stronger attraction than a mere subscription to a magazine. When many persons would not subscribe for the Magazine alone, they will become members because they get two things, the distinction of membership in a well-known society and also a good monthly journal. (529)

In 1904 new members had to be recommended to the society by someone who already belonged. Even advertisers stressed that *Geographic* subscribers were "a class of people distinctly in the higher walks of life."[9] However, as membership grew at a rapid pace, it was difficult to preserve the sense of exclusiveness.

By 1912 Grosvenor and Bell had built a society with thousands of members. From 1888 to 1912, membership had increased from 1,000 to 107,000. Dr. Bell addressed the society in these words: "There never has been in the history of the world a scientific society that has increased in influence and power as the National Geographic Society has."[10] By 1913 there was a growth of 60.5 percent over the preceding year. There were 337,446 members in 1914. By 1936, the society had 5 million members.

The society's membership included not only many of the country's most cultured and substantial people but a large group of citizens possessing only modest education and material advantages. Its funding of research gave its membership a sense of participating in science:

The lonely forest ranger, the clerk at his desk, the plumber, the teacher, the eight year old boy or the octogenarian cannot, like a Carnegie, Rockefeller, Ford, or Guggenheim, send out his own expeditions, but as a member of the National Geographic Society he can enjoy having a part in supporting exploration conducted by his own society and reading the first-hand accounts in his own Magazine. ("NGS," 530)

Constituted through the society's readership was a purportedly more egalitarian "imagined community" that included as members both millionaires and clerks. The *Geographic*'s use of photographs was thought by its editors to put readers of different class and educational backgrounds on the same footing, as it was commonly held that no special training or competence would be needed to either take photographs or read the language of images. The transparency of the photograph, its seeming naturalness, and its potential democratic accessibility were always seen as inseparable, even in 1839, when Daguerre first made public his photographic process by claiming "*anyone* can take the most detailed views in a few minutes by a chemical and physical process which gives nature the ability to reproduce herself."[11] Both photography's automatic nature and its democratic potential were present from the very beginning, and almost immediately its double appeal was exploited. Though little has been written on the part photography played in the development of a so-called egalitarian nationalist discourse, Benedict Anderson's thesis on print culture before the invention of photography anticipates this later moment. Anderson writes of how members' sense of belonging was mediated by participating in a complex set of shared simultaneous events:

> [Print media] creates this extraordinary mass ceremony. . . . Each communicant is well aware that the ceremony he performs is being replicated simultaneously by thousands (or millions) of others whose existence he is confident, yet of whose identity he has not the slightest notion.[12]

The *Geographic* used the democratic rhetoric of photographic images to bring readers into close relation not only to each other but to a more educated community of nationally known scientists and explorers. Members could feel that they belonged to a community through the shared mass experience of looking at photographs in a particular month of every year rather than needing face-to-face contact. In 1912 Bell expressed another more virtuous way society members were linked together through the use of a portion of annual membership fees to sponsor scientific expeditions:

> We have now an annual surplus over and above all the running expenses of the Society, amounting last year to $43,000—a surplus to be devoted to geographic science. Why, that is equivalent to more than 4 percent upon an investment of 1 million dollars. We never had to take off our hats to any multi-millionaire for having endowed the Society with a million dollars; we have done it ourselves.[13]

The National Geographic Society identified the support of its members with acts of philanthropy to such an extent that it thought of itself "not as a commercial enterprise but an altruistic institution . . . the only dividend which it pays is the geographic knowledge it disburses primarily to all its members and secondarily to the world at large."[14] Yet this philanthropic discourse central to the promotion of the *Geographic*'s own myth prevailed more effectively on the level of image than of policy. Despite the use of a portion of annual membership fees to sponsor scientific expeditions, the membership, in fact, was remote from determining the society's program.

Image has a double sense in *National Geographic*'s discourse, both as the kind of magazine that was imagined or fantasized (Is the "image" of the *Geographic* altruistic or commercial? Is it a governmental organization, part of the university, or an elite men's club?) and as the actual representation, the photograph. What the *Geographic* does is make one see the institution of "the Geographic" as inseparable from the literal representation of the image it presents of itself. The photographs of the institution itself are the most obvious example of this. The classical style of architecture of the "home of the National Geographic Society," which one associates with federal buildings as well as with its location in Washington, D.C., the nation's capital, makes one think of the *Geographic* as a government institution. Similarly, the identification of the magazine in *Geographic* photographs with school children and libraries associates it with either public libraries or universities. Such photographs constantly force one to recognize a visual style simultaneously with a type of governmental institution. The two cannot be separated. The image suggests that there is a particular kind of institution in the *National Geographic* we see, whereas, in fact, the *National Geographic* is in the image itself, it is the image—"a surface which suggests nothing but itself, and yet in so far as it suggests there is something behind it, prevents us from considering it as a surface."[15]

So far, I have shown how the *National Geographic* masquerades an image of itself as a governmental discourse and assumes the status of an elite men's club or the authority of a professional geographical institution. It enjoys the privileges of associating itself with all of these fictive identities without actually being any of them. Most striking is how it indulges in these self-images to claim more authority, prestige, and glamour than it would otherwise be entitled to if it presented itself for what it actually is—a commercialized discourse of mass culture.

Colonialist Photography and National Identity

So successful were the *Geographic*'s fictive self-representations that the institution gained a position of enormous power and influence. Indeed, the *Geographic* became one of the principal discursive spaces of the twentieth century in which the United States represented the rest of the world to itself. From its beginnings in the late nineteenth century the magazine played a central role in the production of ideology in connection with a U.S. expansionist project. The Spanish-American War and the closing of the western frontier hastened great change in the national role of the United States. The emergence of the United States as a world power and its interest in having colonies gave a specific purpose to a magazine that enabled readers to visualize spaces that otherwise would have remained inaccessible and remote.

The National Geographic Society was founded in 1888 and evolved slowly until events in 1898 helped accelerate its progress. The Spanish-American War increased the U.S. role in international politics and thus brought world geography to the forefront of the national consciousness. Phillip Pauley cites *Geographic* editor John Hyde, who wrote in May 1899:

> It is doubtful if the study of any branch of human knowledge ever before received so sudden and powerful a stimulus as the events of the past year have given to geography. ("NGS," 521)

After the Spanish-American War, when the potential of geography as a militarily useful study became evident, geography once again became transformed into an active research interest. Articles in the *Geographic* appeared on the geography and commercial potential of so-called U.S. possessions. There was also considerable discussion of the benefits of colonialism. The *National Geographic* magazine became influential through the way it was able to use visual images to connect U.S. colonialism to a project of modernization and progress. U.S. superiority in science and technology was often used as a means to reveal the nation's higher achievements. In the 1907 *National Geographic* article titled "Some Recent Instances of National Altruism: The Efforts of the United States to Aid the Peoples of Cuba, Puerto Rico and the Philippines," evidence of the benefits of U.S. "altruism" in Cuba included cleaning

the squalor and the misery of the prisons ... eliminating the
presence of yellow fever which previously had threatened the health
of this country and ... opening and cleaning the sewers.[16]

Photographs revealed the contrast between Cuba before and Cuba
after U.S. intervention in order to highlight recent improvements.
Similarly, in the pages of *National Geographic* the United States was
sharply differentiated from other countries in the subjects presented,
depicted as a country that had become transformed by the wonders
of modern science, as evidenced in a 1909 *Geographic* article, "The
Call of the West":

> Homes are being made for millions of people in the arid West. The
> American West is no longer a vast wilderness of mountains, deserts
> and plains. Now that irrigation canals have spread wide oases of
> green in the arid desert. Cheerful, prosperous communities dot a
> landscape once vacant and voiceless.[17]

If the United States represented the future, Europe and the rest of the
world represented the past. Rural villages and old quaint towns were
represented shrouded in superstition and ignorance. Once democratic principles and U.S. progress intervened, however, the stigma of
the past could immediately be lifted. In an article titled "The Emancipation of Mohammedan Women," democratic revolutions brought
light and modern education to backward women in Turkey who
"have previously been shrouded in mystery—concealed behind
thick veils and flowing draperies."[18]

National Geographic's dramaturgical project consisted of dispel-
ling the gloom that prevented the full visibility of things, men,
women, and truths in the world. It sought to break up the patches of
darkness that blocked the light, to eliminate the shadowy areas of society and fill them in with its own ethnocentric regime of truth.
Through the belief in the objectivity and impartiality of science and
new photographic technologies, the *National Geographic* was able
to conceive of itself as becoming a great force in the world, and a
particularly effective means to promote U.S. nationalism. In this connection I quote from an editorial in the *Boston Herald* that was reprinted in the February 1913 issue of *National Geographic*:

> Here is an agency the force of which cannot be overstated. Indeed,
> the modern innovation of hatching chickens by incubators instead of
> hens is simply nowhere compared with the system of hatching

patriots of the stamp of William Tell by geological geography, as exemplified in the faith and works of the National Geographic Society of Washington, D.C.

This is no wild paradox. In truth, have not the greatest historians insisted that the reason why there is no such thing as the existence of patriotic sentiment in China is solely due to the fact that the human heart is incapable of loving 400 million fellow creatures one knows nothing about?

They are a pure numerical abstraction to a man. Of their lives, languages, aspirations, joys, and sorrows he is ignorant of every concrete item, unless that they all wear the national pigtail; and so, even this dangling appendage is not potent enough to bind the people together in the chords of universal love.

Just the same used to be asserted of the United States of America. The States were too big, too broadly dispersed, too divergent in interests, for anyone to be capable of loving their multitudinous populations as fellow countrymen. All this, however, at any rate in the eyes of the National Geographic Society of Washington, is now rapidly being done away with. It is getting effected through a vivid appeal to the visual imagination which is enabling us all to see, in the mind's eye, our whole country at once and as a whole. The stupendous national enterprises already completed, or about to be inaugurated are fast annihilating all lines of geographical division, and enlisting the minds and hearts of the scattered millions in vast undertakings in which all share a common interest and common pride.[19]

In this passage the *Geographic* is fantasized as the latest in modern technologies—a fertilizing machine that reproduces identical "patriots of the stamp of William Tell." From such a pre-Benjaminian perspective, machines that mechanically reproduce imaginary images of "a nation as a whole" have an evolutionary significance for the formation of modern nations. The implication is that if machines are functional for chickens and hens, they should be equally functional for human beings. According to this discourse, mechanical reproduction is glorified because it offers an improvement over biological reproduction, for it assures the elimination of internal ethnic differences and diversity among its manufactured "patriots." Like most masculinist texts, this fantasy provides a way for men to compensate for their envy of women's procreative power, by producing their own superior means of reproduction.

It is worth noting that not only women are written out of this text (in this case women's bodies are supplanted altogether in the service of "hatching patriots" for the nation), but so are other non-Western national traditions, which are troped as exclusively male but feminized in terms of the editorial's logic. This thinking is hinted at by inscribing the national pigtail of the Chinese ("a dangling appendage") as the impotent signifier of Chinese masculinity and nationalism.

Embedded in an insult to the Chinese's gender is a myth of the magazine's own masculinist origin and function. The writer sets up an unconscious pattern of relation between Self and Other by comparing the phallic power of an idealized fantasy image of U.S. patriots "hatched by geological geography" to its monstrous negation, 400 million Chinese patriots bonded together by "a national pigtail." Finally, myth and fantasy continually reverse into one another. The Chinese and Americans are both shown as lacking until the arrival of the *National Geographic*, which assures U.S. national superiority through its new visual technologies. U.S. national identity gets expressed in terms of sexual difference: the U.S. patriot with real phallic power (the *National Geographic*) is opposed to his Chinese counterpart, who has merely a feminized substitute, a "national pigtail." The comparison is set up to affirm the superiority of U.S. white masculinity, now marked by technological powers that make it infallible.

Besides offering an example of how a peculiarly U.S. sexist and racist scientific imagination works, I want to point out how this passage raises the serious problem of establishing a common U.S. national identity in a country that is "too big, too broadly dispersed, [and] too divergent in interests." As cultural theorist Phillip Fisher points out:

> Americans were not a Volk. They had no common racial origin and no common history. Open to immigration and flooded by immigrants in the century between 1820 and 1920, they were a patchwork of peoples. In addition, with no shared religion, no deep relation to a common language, no shared customary way of life with its ceremonies and manners, no single style of humor or common inherited maxims and unspoken rules, the continental nation also lacked just those features that any romantic theory of the nation-state required.[20]

Without a common racial origin, history, religion, or language, the national fact of the United States meant that somehow the problem of identity must be solved by other, unprecedented means. This editorial suggests that this was evidently an urgent task at the turn of the century in what was fast becoming a world power. Since Americans did not have any single human feature in common, not even a "national pigtail," something else would have to be invented in order to posit a "community in anonymity," to use Benedict Anderson's words.[21]

According to the *Boston Herald* editorial, the concept of a nation is regarded as both natural and universal. Theorists of nationalism such as Benedict Anderson, however, would argue against such attempts at essentializing it. Anderson sees the nation as an imaginary concept:

> It is imagined because the members of even the smallest nation will never know most of their fellow-members, meet them, or even hear of them, yet in the minds of each lives the image of their communion. (14)

Anderson goes on to point out that "all communities larger than primordial villages of face-to-face contact (and perhaps even these) are imagined" (15). Yet nationalist discourse exists despite its being a fictional idea because it is constituted by other means than face-to-face contact among members. For Anderson, nationalist consciousness in modern societies was dependent on the emergence of newspapers and novels. Through new print technologies a nationalist identity became mechanically reproducible.

The *National Geographic* is a perfect example of what Anderson refers to when he explains that print media became the dominant means for particularizing the social and cultural field of a nation in the modern era.

Armchair Traveling

The *National Geographic* magazine facilitated the imagination of the nation by constructing itself as a historically significant national institution, frequently publishing retrospective accounts of its own history along with statistics that would show the increasing number of subscribers. Occasionally speeches by members would be published to show their participation in its great enterprise. The following statement was made by Dr. Harvey Wiley, a dinner guest at the seventh annual banquet held to celebrate the growth of the *National Geographic* in 1912:

> I am glad that I live in an age when it is not necessary any longer to
> wander into distant regions to learn geography. All we have to do
> now is to sit still in easy chairs and our great men bring the world
> before us. Last year I had the great pleasure of hearing Admiral Peary
> lay bare the secrets of the North Pole in such vivid language and with
> such perfect satisfaction that I at once gave up my desire to visit that
> locality. . . . One week ago tonight I went with Professor Nitobe over
> the whole of that beautiful island of Formosa and saw it in all its
> beauty and grandeur, at a smaller sum than 5 cents. So all that we
> have to do is to sit still and let the world come to us.[22]

What is significant is how the *Geographic*'s image of the nation works paradoxically by claiming to include those more sedentary white, male Americans that otherwise would be excluded from experiencing a masculine adventure and the exotic firsthand. Dr. Wiley was enthralled by the National Geographic Society's lectures because they created a myth of classlessness and agelessness—the idea that, whatever differences existed between men, each had the same access to all the world's peoples and cultures through photography. Thus the causes of class differences, for example, were obscured by offering every member, whether he was a doctor or a Carnegie, equal visual access to brown bodies and the supposed experience of a real adventure. In this way the armchair traveler did not have to give up his middle-class style of comfort in order to experience the privileges of upper-class white masculinity. Differences between classes were less easy to discern, now that photography democratized travel. Not only did Wiley find Peary's vivid language and slides convincing, he found they actually substituted for the experience of exploration itself. For Wiley, representations of exotic places were actually more satisfying than the real thing and thus made traveling superfluous.

In the early days of the society, women were not allowed to attend public meetings and lectures. The experience of armchair travel was an exclusively male arena. Yet this soon changed when through its magazine the experience of its lecture series was eventually made available within the domestic sphere. Women, too, could now enjoy the pleasures of travel without leaving home, and *National Geographic* began to have a place within a wider social order. The following letter sent in by a housewife and published in one of its issues for 1936 attests to the growing importance of the *National Geographic* and its relation to the bourgeois home:

> Whenever things get in a rut, life seems dull, walled in by
> monotonous repetitions or filled with perplexities, I pick up a
> *National Geographic*, sit down and go traveling. I come back
> refreshed, enlightened, and more conscious of the fullness of life —
> and we are very likely to have something different for dinner that
> night.[23]

National Geographic's articles on travel offered the housewife an escape from reality to remote places of the globe and enabled her to enjoy the fantasy position of entering into situations completely different from her own life. The *Geographic* made the housewife happy and productive. It refreshed, enlightened, and inspired her to prepare "something different for dinner that night," but, most importantly, it did so without inspiring her to step out of place and upset the conditions of her everyday life.

Playing a similar role to Hollywood's, the National Geographic Society would entertain its audience by adding the flavor of adventure to an otherwise tasteless recipe of science. Yet instead of fabricating fictions for its audience it would entertain with facts. It would use photographs rather than moving pictures and would feature explorers, travelers, and scientists as its stars rather than actors. Its educational purpose made it morally superior to Hollywood. Yet its subject matter would be equally thrilling. It, too, would make the exotic seem familiar.

What *National Geographic* offered that Hollywood did not was participation. I have already mentioned that the subscribers of the magazine were automatic club members and that their money went directly into club activities. Although most of its members preferred to be armchair travelers, others would one day want to become explorers. *National Geographic* saw that this profession would have a great deal of appeal, especially to men. Its pictures of bare-breasted female ethnographic subjects suggested some of the sensuous rewards of what otherwise might have been conceived of as rather a dull and tedious profession. Science evidently had its privileges outside the home as well. If some did not consider an acting career a manly pursuit, exploration offered an assurance of masculinity. The figure of the explorer came to embody an enviable kind of masculinist identity.

Black Skins, White Photographs: The Configuration of Geographical Desire

In 1896 the *National Geographic* became the first geographic magazine to print photographs of bare-breasted "natives." The first photograph to exemplify what later became a celebrated *Geographic* tradition was also the occasion for humor that, as distasteful as it is now, was intended then to be amusing. Entitled "Zulu Bride and Bridegroom," this photograph connects the couple's dark skin with a savage's disposition:

> These people are of a dark bronze hue, and have good athletic figures. They possess some excellent traits, but are horribly cruel when once they have smelled blood.[24]

In this caption, the deployment of the rhetoric of savagery serves as the necessary foil, the essential opposition, giving substance to the superiority of the civilized white *Geographic* reader. Such images of brown bodies would continue to serve as the territory across which *Geographic* readers claimed their modernity and competed for national superiority. From that period on, the *Geographic* has always been willing to show images of women's breasts in any color, just as long as they were not white. On one occasion, a Polynesian girl appeared suspiciously fair-skinned. According to Melville M. Payne, the president of the society, the problem was taken care of in the *Geographic*'s laboratories: "We darkened her down to make her look more native—more valid, you might say."[25]

Images of partially naked native women in the pages of *National Geographic* was another way that the magazine constituted collective U.S. national experiences through photographs. Of course, at that time the pleasures of this fraternity were mostly enjoyed by white men. Male adolescent fantasies about sex and exploration were expressed in popular films such as Frank Capra's 1940s film *It's a Wonderful Life*:

In the same year that Peary included a conventional pinup image of his mistress in his biography, the *National Geographic* magazine inaugurated a similar practice of presenting bare-breasted women of color as sexual objects. The photograph of the couple identified as a "Zulu Bride and Bridegroom" carried the following caption, which linked people of color with savagery: "These people are of a dark bronze hue, and have good athletic figures. They possess some excellent traits, but are horribly cruel when once they have smelled blood."

You don't like coconuts? Don't you know where coconuts come from? Lookee here. From Tahiti, the Fiji Islands, the Coral Sea. A new magazine—only us explorers can get it. I've been nominated for membership in the National Geographic Society. I'm going out exploring some day. You and I are going to have a couple of harems maybe and three to four wives. Wait and see.

Journalist Tom Buckley, recalling his favorite *Geographic* photograph of "an exceptionally nubile, perhaps Nubian, young woman" who was identified as "a Sudanese slave girl, the property of an Arab merchant," remarked in 1970 that it was her pose, "her shoulders thrown back in proud servility," that made this image, as he put it, "the stuff of multidimensional sexual fantasy beside whom the girls in *Playboy* are poor plastic things indeed."[26] Native subordination and servility, old staples of colonial discourse, provide libidinal excitation for Buckley, even in 1970.

Without discomfort or expense, male members of the National Geographic Society were able to claim a proprietary interest in the women of countries that remained outside U.S. boundaries. Undoubtedly such power relations were shaped within the sexual politics of looking, structured by relations of gender, class, and race that became peculiar to a U.S. tradition. These hierarchies, however, were hidden by the *Geographic* magazine's own faith in its verbal and visual authority and the power of neutral observation. In 1903 Alexander Graham Bell claimed that "prudery should not influence the decision of printing photographs of half-naked Philippine Island natives."[27]

By claiming that photographs showed things as they were, the underlying structure of gender, class, and race relations that determined the *Geographic*'s policy of voyeurism was never called into question. Grosvenor defended Bell's decision on the grounds that "the pictures were a *true* reflection of the times in those islands" (89). Grosvenor's appeal to photography's purported truthfulness lent authority to his essential opposition of a representative nonwestern, black, primitive "them" to a monolithic U.S., white, educated "us." This "us/them" structure was productive in terms of establishing an imagined and imaginary national community of *Geographic* readers that was otherwise fragmented along lines of gender, race, and class.

The National Geographic Society had the image of an exclusive private men's club, yet the membership was mostly from the middle class. What was preserved as the sign of a certain kind of upper-class male privilege were photographs of sexually explicit non-Western women. These were presented to show that it was acceptable for men to fantasize about engaging in extramarital sexual relations. Even *National Geographic* advertisers integrated some erotic strategies and used photographs of women of color as sexually available as part of their ad campaigns. In one 1911 ad for a train company, the photograph of a partially veiled woman staring at the viewer with a look of urgent availability is accompanied by the caption "Mention the Geographic—It identifies you."[28]

Such ads fed on fantasy and a longing to construct an imagined and imaginary community of *Geographic* readers that tapped into a life-style that was openly elitist and at odds with the values of its actual middle-class readership. The creation of such images of non-white women in sexually suggestive poses made it possible for male readers to experience through these photographs, albeit fictionally, a shared commonality with the wealthy and influential male writer-explorers of the *National Geographic*, thus creating a site for the possibility of a gendered community of readers who shared, in Anderson's terms, a "deep, horizontal comradeship."[29]

The Metaphor of White Heroism: Vagaries of the Male Body

In the *Geographic,* access to technology was a source of peaceful freedom that gave the illusion of risk but actually did not make men give up anything in order to participate—least of all their own lives. It is significant that death is completely absent from *Geographic*'s discourse. When well-known explorers die in action, the *Geographic* seldom notifies the public. For example, the only reference to the death of British Capt. Robert Falcon Scott appears in a caption of a photograph several years later. The image of the Scott expedition taken before Scott's death is one that connotes action rather than impotence or death.[30] In order for exploration to be kept in line with dominant ideas of masculinity as activity, it was first necessary to conceal all elements of passivity or failure. In a similar way the images of Robert Peary in the *National Geographic* would never have told us

Santa Fe de-Luxe

The only extra-fare train to California—extra fast and extra fine

California Limited

Also exclusively for first-class travel
Fred Harvey dining-car meals
On the way visit the world-wonder
Grand Canyon of Arizona
For art booklets of both trains address W.J.Black, Pass.Traffic Mgr.
A.T.& S.F.Ry. System, 1072 Railway Exchange, Chicago

Santa Fe
All the way

COPYRIGHT W.J.BLACK, 1911

"Mention the Geographic—It identifies you."

The advertisements in *National Geographic* followed a similar strategy to that of the magazine's picture stories. Brown female bodies were used to serve as the territory across which advertisers could claim their modernity as evidenced in this "Santa Fe de-Luxe California Limited" advertisement, which appeared on the back of the October 1911 issue.

what Matthew Henson's autobiography admitted about Peary: that he was passive, literally a dead weight on his return from the pole.[31]

In *National Geographic* the white race is represented as the natural ruler of the globe. Confidence in the invulnerability of this position is constantly reinforced by the *Geographic*'s fictionalized construct of white men as heroes marked by technological powers. As I pointed out in the previous chapter, many of the stories about Peary are built around ritualized scenes, all of which are devoid of genuine suspense. He always accomplishes what he is after, whether it entails an adventure on the Greenland ice cap or an expedition to the North Pole, where he conquers the forces of nature to reach the "top of the earth." In *National Geographic* Peary and other explorers appear always to return intact with photographs that serve as proof of their hardships and struggles, and as trophies of their masculinity. Although Peary is the subject and agent of his narratives, he rarely appears in the photographs that document his stories. Controlling the look, he leaves himself out of the pictures. The photographs of his expedition are often of women and the Inuit people that were the work force of his expedition. His body is exempted from scrutiny because it is taken for granted, whereas the Eskimo people are extensively defined and photographed. Sexual and social meanings are imposed on their bodies, not on that of the white man.[32]

National Geographic accounts of Peary are shot through with an obsession with images and definitions of white masculinity and masculine codes of behavior. What is particularly important is that the bodies never show any signs either of wounds or of blood. We are never told about the odd limb that is blasted off, the toes that Peary lost from frostbite.

Although the stories are often narratives of male combat, direct displays of Peary's white male body tend to be fairly brief. The occlusion of the white explorer's body is intensified with the deployment of new technologies of transport and communication in the polar regions a decade after Peary's exploits. The replacement of dogs and sledges with radios and airplanes in the 1920s had paradoxical consequences for the image and discourse of male heroism. Indeed, the discourses of science and technology of the 1920s alter the function of the polar explorer. The concept of *explorer* was no longer connected with the notion of a vocation—learning the tradition of his craft, gaining an individuated view of that tradition through a process that sometimes took practically an entire lifetime to achieve. By the 1920s, however, this older style of exploration becomes problematized when both knowledge, which becomes increasingly specialized, and experience, which is intimately tied to the machine, alter in relation to the change in exploration itself. Once science had penetrated and polar exploration held less risk, women too were possible agents, as Lt. Comm. Richard Byrd acknowledges:

> Here we come to a very interesting thing about Arctic exploration by air. Hundreds of people, men and women, volunteered to go. We could have recruited an army of assistants. . . .
> We received many letters also from people who had no chance to go with us. One letter from a lady—young or old I do not know— was typical. "Little do you realize," she writes, "that thousands of people who have no chance of adventure live your adventure with you. Probably you have no idea what pleasure you give us."[33]

In this period in which Amelia Earhart flies across the Atlantic, white women are able to imagine themselves in the heroic position of the white men that they read about in *National Geographic*. Discourses of science and technology make an earlier form of travel and exploration safe for women to participate in. Yet whether the passing of an older form of explorer makes the new heroes appear less manly is never questioned in the pages of the *Geographic*. The advances in polar exploration are celebrated as technological achievements. The airplane is represented as taking the misery out of an earlier form of polar exploration and for this reason seems to be praised. Also, such achievements bring ordinary readers closer to imagining themselves in these heroic roles.

In "The First Flight to the North Pole," for example, Lt. Commander Byrd recounts that he did not have to suffer any great hardships. Nor did he have to remain alone or rely on human agency to succeed. By applying "Navy training" to aviation, he was able to achieve in one day what seventeen years earlier took Peary a lifetime:

> We discovered no land near the pole. We made no aeronautical records of altitude or duration. We did not suffer any extraordinary hardships, nor can we claim any great personal achievement. We simply took advantage of the knowledge gained by three centuries of Arctic heroes and applied our Navy training to aviation, that great

science born in this country, and so added a short paragraph to the story of man's conquest of the globe on which we live. (357)

Byrd's achievement represents the fruits of earlier explorers' toils. Peary paved the way for Byrd, who in 1926 is able to travel to the region without much risk. Byrd's alliance with science serves a civilizing function in Byrd's narrative, for it spares him and his companion from danger. They will no longer encounter risk from environmental obstacles. Mastery of their machines will ensure them safety. Once Byrd is able to put his airplane in good working order he is able to carry out his adventure without distraction. Mastery of his machines will ensure his safety, for if he is 2,000 feet in the air, the ice can no longer open up beneath him and swallow him into the black waters of the polar sea:

> Within an hour of taking the air we passed the rugged and glacier-laden land and crossed the edge of the polar ice pack. . . . We looked ahead at the ice pack, gleaming in the rays of the midnight sun—a fascinating scene whose lure had drawn famous men into its clutches, never to return. It was with a feeling of exhilaration that we felt that for the first time in history two mites of men could gaze upon her charms, and discover her secrets, out of reach of those sharp claws. (365)

Nature coded as feminine has yielded completely to the dominating presence of Western technological male. Thus the effect of investing domination with libidinal intensities no longer holds any risks. Byrd and Floyd Bennett claim to feel exhilarated at being safely removed from nature, so that they could "gaze upon her charms, and discover her secrets, out of reach of those sharp claws." However, this sensation also seemed to be combined with something else—some sort of nondistinction between being active and passive. Metamorphosed into their instruments, Byrd and Bennett represent themselves as objects perfectly obedient to the mechanical laws of movement. As explorers, they become no more than their machine's trajectory:

> We felt no larger than a pinpoint and as lonely as the tomb; as remote and detached as a star.
> Here, in another world, far from the herds of people, the smallness of life fell from our shoulders. What wonder that we felt no great emotion of achievement or fear of death that lay stretched beneath us, but instead, impersonal, disembodied. On, on we went. It seemed forever onward. (376)

As technology advances *National Geographic* heroes become more passive, fascinated, and silent—features usually used to describe women in the presence of men. Pleasure is aligned with death rather than with life. Byrd and Bennett "felt no great emotion or fear of death . . . but instead, impersonal, disembodied."

After Richard Byrd's 1929 flight over the pole by airplane, in 1959 a group of U.S. scientists traveled under the North Pole in a nuclear submarine in the last polar trek to use advanced technology. As outer space and the moon became the new privileged sites of technological progress, the poles ceased to be a representation of the future. Although there were attempts to reach the pole after 1959, these returns were predominantly symptoms of nostalgia for a type of exploration that had passed. Obsolete forms of technologies were now applied to polar exploration. In the polar trek of 1986, a team of U.S. explorers traveled to the North Pole using low-tech dog sleds and cross-country skis. In this recent polar revival, polar exploration becomes associated with a pastoral nostalgia.

By 1959 the *Geographic*'s "heroes" are no longer polar explorers but astronauts. The moon and the planets are now the testing ground for the project of science. The recent shift in new technologies of transport and communication has intensified contradictions already present between male heroism and male dependence on technology, resulting in a significantly greater gap between the ideal of male heroism and the material experience. The most striking formulation is given by Tom Wolfe, who in his book *The Right Stuff* suggests that the *Mercury* astronauts, though they were presented to the public as great pilots, were more like "test subjects," interchangeable with trained chimpanzees:

> Control—in the form of overrides at the very least—was the one thing that would neutralize the recurring taunt within the fraternity: "A monkey's gonna make the first flight." In his speech before the brotherhood Slayton had brought that out into the open with his crack about the "college-trained chimpanzee."[34]

Wolfe explains that there was nothing secret about the fact that such a "college" actually existed. The apes had begun their training at the same time as the astronauts, in the late spring of 1959. Wanting to be treated like pilots in control, as opposed to chimpanzees, the astronauts demanded from the scientists who designed the rockets that a window be installed in space capsules. Wolfe describes the action the astronauts took against the scientists:

> The seven men pressed on. They were tired of the designation of "capsule" for the Mercury vehicle. The term as much as declared that the man inside was not a pilot but an experimental animal in a pod. . . . As it was now designed, the Mercury capsule had no window, just a small porthole on either side of the astronaut's head. His main way of seeing the outside world would be through a periscope. Now the astronauts insisted on a window. . . . And why? Because pilots had windows in their cockpits and hatches they could open on their own. That was what it was all about: being a pilot as opposed to a guinea pig. (160)

The engineers responded to the astronauts' demands and designed a window. Even if putting a window in rockets could not make astronauts more than passive observers, it would at least elevate them to the position of scientists, given the emphasis on the triumph of the visible within the language of scientific discourse.

By the time men were put into space, exploration of the remote corners of the earth no longer offered the challenges and struggles of an earlier age. Indeed, the contemporary interest up to the present day in *Geographic* polar exploration has reflected a nostalgia for an earlier age when men were real men. It also has allowed for a revisionist history of this earlier period that includes nonwhite male participants that were formerly denied entry into the subject position of exploration narratives. Matthew Henson, the African American man that accompanied Robert Peary to his farthest navigational points, has been the subject of a recent attempt to rewrite the discovery of the North Pole in the pages of *National Geographic*. Despite the so-called egalitarian rhetoric of the *Geographic* during its early days, the "imagined community" constituted by the *Geographic*'s discourse is inflected by distinct representations of gender, race, and class that became peculiar to a U.S. national tradition.

3

White Fade-out?
Heroism and the *National Geographic* in the Age of Multiculturalism

Much of *National Geographic*'s history and discourse turns on the question of "whiteness" as an unmarked category. Now, white values still inform the cultural practices and policies of institutions such as the *National Geographic*. Though white power and dominance is hard to grasp, one of the ways it makes itself felt is by the way white institutions pass themselves off as embodied in the normal. According to cultural critic Coco Fusco:

> Racial identities are not only black, Latino, Asian, Native American and so on; they are also white. To ignore white ethnicity is to redouble its hegemony by naturalizing it. Without specifically addressing white ethnicity, there can be no critical evaluation of the construction of the other.[1]

In his 1988 *Screen* article entitled "White," Richard Dyer inaugurates a shift on the part of white critics by addressing the reorientation of ethnicity that Coco Fusco, among others, calls for.[2] Dyer shows how elusive white ethnicity is as a representational construct, noting that "whiteness often has been taken to be the norm, that is, what passes itself off as if it is the most natural, inevitable and ordinary."[3] Dyer further elaborates on how whiteness is often embedded in an everyday discourse of common sense, thus obscuring its location within a discourse of ethnic difference:

> The very terms we use to describe the major ethnic divide presented

by Western society, "black" and "white," are imported and naturalized by other discourses. Thus it is said (even in liberal texts) that there are inevitable associations of white with light and therefore safety, and black with dark and therefore danger. . . . People point to the Judeo-Christian use of white and black, to symbolize good and evil, as evidenced in such expressions as a "black mark," "white magic," "to blacken the character" and so on. (45)

Dyer observes that whiteness has had an additional appeal as the unmarked category of the "people" in terms of the language of the "nation," which promoted a sense of community and collective identity. Dyer quotes Paul Gilroy, who critiques "the idea of the nation" in the British context as homogeneous:

There is a problem in these plural forms: who do they include, or, more precisely for our purposes, do they help to reproduce blackness and Englishness as mutually exclusive categories? . . . why are contemporary appeals to the "people" in danger of transmitting themselves as appeals to the white people? (45-46)

The rhetoric of the nation, although it permits a wide appeal in terms of "we" and "us," masks whiteness as itself a category. In the context of the *Geographic*, one of the ways we notice that the United States is racially marked as white is by the way social groups that are not American are represented as colored. I will argue that this comparative element seems peculiar to the *Geographic* to this day, as internal ethnic differences continue to be disavowed within the U.S. national imaginary.

The 1988 *National Geographic* video *The Explorers: A Century of Discovery*, which celebrates the National Geographic's one hundredth anniversary, provides an excellent illustration of how the institution narrates the contemporary idea of an imagined United States as being American, white, and male and how this is built on both the circulation of white U.S. explorers in the so-called third world and the circulation of photographs of brown bodies in the first world.[4] In the *Geographic*'s nationalist discourse, external "otherness" provides a unifying model whereby U.S. identity becomes aware of itself as a self by perceiving its difference from non-U.S., nonwhite "others." The video not only constructs a national identity that is white and male through the mass circulation of images of the colonial "other" (brown bodies), but, oddly enough, this identity still remains unproblematically white even as U.S. women and men of color are now incorporated into its narrative of Western heroism.

This leads me to conclude with an example of how a monocultural organization like the Geographic makes gestures toward adopting a superficially multicultural identity through paying homage during its centennial celebration to a token African American explorer, Matthew Henson. I will argue that though the current rearrangement of the North Pole story in the 1988 and 1990 issues of the *National Geographic* magazine accepts Henson as Peary's "companion" rather than as his "servant," this shift in discourse represents more the ploys of a multicultural policy than a socially conscious institutional engagement.

A Video History

The Explorers: A Century of Discovery is a representative product of the National Geographic television and video series SPECIALS, which presents entertainment films that are also educational, dealing with supposedly serious real-world historical events with all the bravado and dash of Hollywood adventure films.[5] This particular tape is both a celebration-cum-advertisement of the hundred-year-old institution, as well as a U.S. colonial adventure film, offering the standard narrative pleasures of adventure through the spectator's identification with the various Geographic heroes represented. A sound track that seems to be extracted from the film *Ben-Hur* along with the authoritative voice-over of the narrator E. G. Marshall, provides an account of famous clips that include images of men and women explorers— Robert Peary, Osa and Martin Johnson, Robert Leakey, Jane Goodall, and others—who became household names through their affiliation in part with the National Geographic Society. The ideal viewer, a member of the National Geographic Society (the tape is only available to members), is drawn into the tape's narrative of U.S. nationalism through identification with the changing figures of U.S. heroes, whose adventures and personal growth are occasioned, even made possible, through the process of U.S. outreach to the so-called third world.

The Explorers: A Century of Discovery opens by presenting a recent event commemorating the history of the National Geographic Society. Offscreen narration accompanying the visuals describes the scene as follows:

> In Washington, D.C., the trustees of the National Geographic Society gather to get a formal portrait taken. The picture will help celebrate the Society's centennial. In 1988 the Geographic completes 100 years of exploration, research, and education.

The voice-over disappears in order for the viewer to overhear the exchange between the photographer and the society's trustees on location in Washington, D.C. This momentary shift in the text's point of view enables the viewer to participate in an institutional event rather than to witness it at a distance. Yet as soon as the photographer pushes down the shutter of his camera, the image shifts from color to black and white and we witness the same event taking place seventy-five years earlier. The voice-over returns to connect the two images:

> Here in 1913 a similar photo was taken. Back then the highest mountain had yet to be climbed and no one knew the ocean deep or what fire illuminates the stars. All this lay in the future—the greatest adventure mankind had ever known.

This precredit sequence alludes to the triumphant narrative of technological progress. To fill in briefly the time gap in photographic and scientific progress between the two portraits, the sequence is followed by a series of filmic snapshots from the most memorable events in the hundred-year history of the National Geographic Society. Similar to classic Hollywood-style vignettes used to identify key actors, these clips provide a preview of the *Geographic* heroes and their great deeds, which will be represented later for the viewer in greater length. The sequence culminates with a freeze-frame that isolates the National Geographic Society's logo—a unified global image. The final credits emerge from this unitary image, which serves as an icon for the way the *Geographic* sees itself as the defining world order in terms of a narrative of scientific progress.

After the fade, the viewer meets the society's founding father, Alexander Graham Bell, and his family; Bell's daughter married Gilbert Grosvenor, who later took over the responsibility of editor of the magazine. Our acquaintance with the *Geographic* family leads to an account of the *Geographic*'s hundred-year history, which is narrated by the offscreen voice of E. G. Marshall. In the telling of this story, the narration directs the viewer, explaining the visuals and offering the sense of history, context, or perspective needed. This arrangement is occasionally interrupted, as in the opening scene when the text shifts to a cinema verité style that enables the viewer to overhear directly the characters in the scene. Such instances, in which synchronous dialogue is produced under location conditions, give the viewer the effect of an eyewitness account of events. Though this approach appears more realistic or natural in terms of letting the viewer come to conclusions about the scene without the intervention of commentary, such a strategy is also problematic. Visuals stand as unquestioned real evidence, rather than as highly mediated representations, even though video representations involve just as much artifice as does any other mode of visual representation. Nevertheless, this video offers its images up as in some sense real, embodying a particular kind of truth, and says to the spectator that you need make no effort to understand this. Drawing on the ideology of the visible as evidence, the tape claims to tell it as it is and offers its version of the hundred years of *Geographic* history as a truthful record rather than as a subjective interpretation.

The Heroic Eye

The Explorers: A Century of Discovery includes various scenes in which the shutter of the camera exactly corresponds to the eyes of the explorer looking at a landscape, person, or city. In each case, after a quick flash to the intensely fixed expression of an explorer, the scene dissolves into a long take that documents the remote landscape, the lost city, or the non-Western person never before seen by Western eyes.

The use of cinematic dissolve in this instance performs important work in the video's narrative. The explorer's gaze is the sign of an explorer's genius. Within the narrative it transforms the unknown into a new reality. Often the camera and the eye of the explorer are conflated not only through the use of dissolves but by the voice-over of the narrative itself: "At the turn of the century the eye of the camera was capable of wondrous revelations." The camera serves a significant function, and I would argue that it is the actual hero of the video, as its mediating function serves to make the explorer *capable* of the act of creation itself. Once legitimized in terms of his particular relation to photographic technology, the explorer can claim complete authoritativeness for his vision. The tape's voice-over tells us that the project of *Geographic* explorers and photographers is to document "the world and all that is in it." Yet the idea that there might be constraints on the explorer's interpretive capacities is never suggested. Instead, the camera as an observation site works as a validating and naturalizing scaffold in the video that confers upon the figure of the explorer an invisibility and all-seeing knowledge that make him or her appear outside of society and history—without nationality, gender, race, or class. The camera, while itself everywhere and nowhere, establishes the videotape's universalist white character and its transcendental white vision.[6]

Race and Gender in the "*Geographic* Tradition"

One of the more disturbing traditions that the *National Geographic* has always upheld is the objectification of the figure of the third-world woman through her eroticization.[7] In chapter 2 I have pointed-ed out how images of partially naked native women in the pages of the *National Geographic* were another way that the magazine constituted U.S. national sexual experiences through photographs. Needless to say, the pleasures of this community were enjoyed almost exclusively by a fraternity of white men. The tape's voice-over makes reference to this magazine's policy of representing nakedness, referred to as "a famous *Geographic* tradition." The celebrated 1896 photograph is reproduced in the videotape with the explanation that "Grosvenor stoutly defended the policy of showing people dressed or undressed according to the customs of their land." Native traditions and photographic accuracy are given as a rationale to support a particular definition of nation, ethnicity, and sexuality in which being "American" is being one of "us"—white and male—as opposed to one of "them"—nonwhite and female.

The next part of the tape's narrative focuses on the properly equipped early twentieth-century Western explorer, who is packed with both guns and cameras to remote places on the planet to claim previously unknown sights for Western civilization. Two such figures in the tape "typifying a new breed of showman explorers . . . equally famous and equally skilled with guns and their many cameras" are a couple, Osa and Martin Johnson, who attempt to "enlighten" U.S. audiences by photographing the "Dark Continent."[8] In the video we see the original black-and-white footage of an unidentified film-maker who captured the Johnsons' reencounter with Africa from the air. Naked African men are depicted jumping up and down as the Johnsons descend from their airplane to greet them. Once this initial scene is recorded by the anonymous "eye of the camera," the explorers literally replace the people that they find there. In the narrative Africa is no longer the continent belonging to its indigenous population but, in the words of the tape, "the natural habitat of the great explorers." A Eurocentric paradigm of modernization and progress is projected onto Africa, legitimizing the U.S. presence by showing how savage and underdeveloped its peoples are in comparison with the Americans. In the black-and-white footage Osa and Martin Johnson arrive on the "Dark Continent" by airplane as the voice of Martin Johnson explains:

> I decided this time to do the Dark Continent in a real modern way—inside two big airplanes capable of landing on either water or land. Pygmies appeared from behind every tree and tuft of grass. A surging, jumping multitude of tiny savages. The happiest people in the world doing their best to show us how overjoyed they were to find us once more in their country after three years' absence.

Johnson's paternalistic rhetoric suggests a certain kind of invulnerability. His physical distance from the natives and his reliance on modern technologies such as the airplane, the camera, and the gun, however, indicate an underlying insecurity. The anxiety abates at a later point when Martin and Osa Johnson are seen dancing to "modern" jazz with the "boy and girl savages." Johnson comments on the scene:

> I said to Osa, let's give the boys and girls some modern jazz. Most savages are greatly puzzled by the phonograph, but the childlike pygmies accept it without curiosity as just another wonder of the white man.

The Johnsons' image of the Africans as childlike and in awe of the white man and his machines (signified by the phonograph and modern music) is an old strategy Westerners have had for interpreting the other as living in a quaint but irrelevant past, actually in need of the

West's intervention to bring them culturally up-to-date.[9] It is significant that in this segment Osa Johnson, a white woman explorer, is represented as bringing African American music via "white" technology to civilize "savage" Africans.

The figure of the white woman also presents a domestic image and indicates a shift in the project of the *National Geographic*, signaling that wild Africa has now been tamed and is thus safe for white women. The image of Osa Johnson dancing with black African men suggests a different form of inequality that emphasizes gender and is reminiscent of other colonial images of white femininity surrounded by male servants of color. In this allegory of empire, the surface gaiety masks the sober meaning behind the image: the U.S. wife's "duty" to teach the "Africans" for their own good the white culture of the West. The gender difference, however, does not make Osa appear less complicitous than her husband is with the ideology of racism. Indeed, here she is even more shameless than her husband as she freely appropriates other cultural traditions — such as the music of African Americans — and presents them under the guise of a white tradition—white because it is made available through U.S. technology. It must be admitted that this is a strange kind of inadvertent indictment of the white woman as colonizer, one bound up, too, with the *National Geographic*'s own sexism.

Yankee Know-how and Scenes of Underdevelopment

In the videotape's more contemporary episodes of *Geographic* history, external otherness continues to bind an ethnically undifferentiated U.S. identity. Throughout the tape the white hero remains the central reference point, but his stature now grows as he appropriates skills from other cultures and uses them as a means to preserve superiority while traveling abroad. Such knowledge, according to the tape, functions as a form of protection in foreign regions of the world that at any moment could prove hostile to a white U.S. presence. This is made very convincing by the example of botanist Joseph Rock, who utilized non-Western skills of survival and is depicted by the video's visuals as performing dazzling escapes in his travels in China and Tibet, where he was often menaced by "bandits and warlords." (In one such episode he is shown ferrying his party across "the raging Yangtze river" with a raft made by local peasants of inflated goat skins.) The tape's commentary is filled with simplistic yet powerful dualisms that establish a reductivist framework in which we can assume that Rock innocently got himself into situations of rivalry where he had to display his cunning against "bloodthirsty rebels" or evil Tibetan kings offering him deadly delicacies like "ancient yak cheese and mutton crawling with maggots."

The metaphor of innocence is important, especially because Rock's reasons for traveling to China and Tibet are not elaborated upon. Instead, these countries are denied a history and function merely as exotic backdrops for Rock to display his superior humanity over a presence described as alien rather than native to the country where the action takes place. Rock's presence is thus never viewed as strange or unwelcome. Rather, as a representative figure of a "good" colonial society, his innocence is assumed. It is the other that is always at fault for upsetting the smooth run of Rock's caravan. Yet these interruptions are never especially worrisome to Rock, who usually escapes in such an orderly fashion that he is often left with extra time to photograph his enemies as well as his escapes. As viewers, we are made into unwitting bystanders drawn into Rock's drama by the eyewitness account displayed before us, described in one case as follows by the tape's voice-over:

> Once Rock was trapped between bloodthirsty rebels on one side and the raging Yangtze river on the other. Local peasants came to help. Supported by inflated goat skins they tried to ferry Rock's party across the Yangtze. Carried a mile downstream, Rock and his caravan escaped unharmed.

The use of documentary film footage presents events as natural and real in a way that is virtually unassailable as a result of the special authority given to documentary representations. This was particularly the case in the 1920s, when filmic images were thought of as being the most transparent and truthful. It is significant that in such early black-and-white newsreels, the whole discourse of white heroism depended upon the silence of nonwhite peoples. Labeled as primitive and savage, those treated as others are shown incapable of participating in the production of representation themselves. Such a rationale can also serve as a justification for their lack of participation in such matters as the authorship of photographic texts.[10]

A similar strategy continues to inform the *Geographic*'s recent reporting on the so-called third world. This newer version retains the metaphor of innocence but replaces an older narrative of adventure with a more feminizing narrative of medical care in which the figure of the white woman is now authorized to administer scientific aid. Such an example is illustrated in the tape's focus on the "primitive" Hogahai, a group of people living in the remote highlands of Papua New Guinea. The tape's voice-over explains how the colonialist come-and-help-us mentality seems to justify a more feminized U.S. interventionist policy now:

> Until a few years ago no outsiders knew of their existence, and they have been so isolated that they have not developed antibodies to protect them against common diseases. Not long ago the Hogahai realized that they were dying out, so they forsook their isolation and sent five men to the outside world to ask for help.

This voice-over is an example of ventriloquism in which the other is made to speak the speech of the colonizer. Thus, indirect discourse is used to present the figure of Carol Jenkins, a medical anthropologist brought in by the *Geographic* as a savior rather than an intrusive presence. The protection of the Hogahai becomes a signifier for the continuation of *Geographic*'s imperialist project in the present. Even as the white woman is figured as establishing and maintaining order, she is presented in a feminized role. Placed in the position of a mother protecting her children, she by her presence brings white women to cultural power not as autonomous agents but by virtue of their biological sex. By representing Dr. Jenkins primarily as nursing Hogahai infants, the visuals project into the past the features of the present, replacing a woman's function as doctor with an image of maternal femininity in order to insist that historically produced social roles are timeless and still biologically determined.[11]

Significantly, this is the only contemporary segment of the tape that focuses strictly on people, rather than on nature or (as in the search for "man's origins" by Dr. Leakey) skeletons. These other areas of scientific interest tend to efface the native inhabitants in order to display uninhabited nature. In segments on the Brazilian tropical rain forest, Brazilian Indians are included only as a means to supply a kind of exotic local color. This forest is not acknowledged as a part of Brazil, but rather as a "natural resource" for Western industrial chemicals, drugs, and food. A similar perspective is presented in a segment on Dian Fossey, who died in Africa trying to save the mountain gorillas from extinction.[12] Natives of the region are presented only as savage poachers responsible for murdering innocent and wild creatures.

If Western anthropologists and biologists are depicted as heroes and heroines, they no longer have to fight off hostile natives to survive but are now welcomed messengers of Western science. The other major change is that, unlike earlier *Geographic* stories, contemporary white women are now included as active agents of its discourse. *Geographic* heroism remains a white concept, though it is no longer an all-male preserve. Given the *Geographic*'s tradition of excluding white women, however, it is understandable that one might be suspicious of the frequency of representations of white women in the more contemporary segments. The *Geographic* might want to distinguish its past from its present by way of using white women in its contemporary segments as transmitters of U.S. science. Also, adding women to exploration enables the society to appear as if it has shifted the paradigm of exploration and science away from the structural sexism of its past.

Whitewashing Colonialism

As time passes in the cinematic narrative, what remains constant is the National Geographic Society's erasure of the relations of violence and domination that provide its historic and its psychic armature. This enables it to whitewash its colonial past to perpetuate a continuous discourse in the present under a more benevolent gaze, either feminine or aesthetic. What also remains constant is the National Geographic Society's excuse that non-Western cultures and territories need the scientific expertise of *Geographic* explorers/scientists/photographers to intercede on their behalf, to save peoples and animals from extinction, and to preserve the beauty of nature and protect it from destructive human demands.

As the "great discoveries" of the last hundred years of *Geographic* explorations unfold in chronological order, the voice-over alerts us to an internal evolution toward the aesthetic operating in the later narrative. The arrival of the art photographer signals an advance over the figure of the explorer at a moment when "there were few places on Earth that man did not conquer. . . . With the triumph at Mount Everest in 1954 . . . a romantic venture of high adventure had ended":

> This too is an explorer. The man with a camera explores the subtle play of light and emotion as dawn breaks over a remote town in Turkey. Jim Stanfield is a *National Geographic* staff photographer, a job many covet but few could endure.
>
> Stanfield usually works alone. For eight to nine months of the year his home is the world and his eyes belong to the magazine. Stanfield usually works alone not just for convenience but to leave his mind and heart bare—open to his subjects. When an artist of any kind looks at his subjects he looks at them with everything that he is, so his knowledge and his experience enable him to relate to that subject and produce more meaningful and sensitive work.

The filmic images accompanying the voice-over show Jim Stanfield, alone, perched above his object of vision. Relations of dominance and possession are articulated by his possession of the camera, which slants the balance of power in his favor. Like the Johnsons, Stanfield can create aesthetic meaning out of the Turkish peoples' incongruities, asymmetries, and local color. This film clip of Jim Stanfield at works shows us the power of the enlightened Western artist to salvage the beauty of non-Western peoples and to enshrine it in a racially marked discourse of Western creativity and worth. Stanfield's intervention as an "artist of the camera" is crucial to the *Geographic*'s current curatorial role in culture, producing and ensuring particular constructions of non-Western culture for the consumption of the West.

By concluding the *Geographic*'s canon of great explorers with the figure of the photographer as an artist, the video succeeds in affirming several things. This sequence omits past tensions and controversies, a circumstance that works to recognize retrospectively the *Geographic*'s previous explorers as great men who will survive the test of time. This result might not otherwise be certain, as the claims of some of the early explorers were controversial. Such was the case of Robert Peary, the first explorer in this videotape's evolutionary line of *Geographic* heroes. However, the tape's voice-over washes out the more explicit references to colonial exploitation and racism in the early *Geographic* accounts that represent the Inuit peoples and an African American man, Matthew Henson, as "cogs" that were instrumental to the workings of what Peary termed his well-managed "traveling machine." In this revised version Matthew Henson is no longer a mere cog but "a pioneering black explorer who was Peary's closest associate." Peary's bald exploitation of the Eskimos also disappears in this account. Instead we learn that "he lived with the Eskimos and became accepted as one of them."

Reinscribing Peary in the World

The power of this discourse is indicated in Wally Herbert's 1988 article, "Did Peary Reach the Pole?" which effaces the social relations of discovery even as it contests the accuracy of Peary's claims. Herbert's article makes an unsuccessful attempt to shift the norms of white heroism away from deeds to intent, yet this does not lead him to question the race and gender relations of Peary's expedition (see chapter 1). Even though Herbert shows that Peary failed from a scientific perspective, he retells the story of Peary's last expedition as a positive measure of his creativity and worth. Thus it is Peary the pioneer, the hero who "extended" the "bounds of human endeavor," that Herbert celebrates:

> As to whether or not Peary reached the North Pole, the answer, by the nature of the subject elements within it, can never be anything more than a probability. Regardless of the answer, from the higher ground of history Peary stands out as a pioneer who contributed to mankind. Impelled by the energy of his obsession, conquering with his exceptional courage man's fear of the unknown, he extended the bounds of human endeavor. Thus was his mission a success.[13]

Herbert's metaphor of Peary as a seer who conquers man's fear of the unknown perpetuates the illusion that there is such a thing as freedom from the world and nourishes the humanist's notion of freedom of spirit. Such a dogma is itself a determined and determining gesture that conveniently advocates an aestheticization of life outside of the world of brutality and exploitation that Peary lived and participated in. In order to inscribe Peary back into the very text of the world, I will briefly include another perspective on Peary, this time from an elderly man in Siorapaluk, who gave the following account of Peary's encounter with the Inuit people. The following quotation appeared in Kenn Harper's book *Give Me My Father's Body: The Life of Minik, the New York Eskimo*, published in 1986. The quote resulted from an interview Harper had with an Inuit man in 1967:

> People were afraid of him . . . really afraid. . . . His big ship . . . it made a big impression on us. He was a great leader. You always had the feeling that if you didn't do what he wanted, he would condemn you to death. . . . I was very young, but I will never forget how he treated the Inuit. . . . His big ship arrives in the bay. He is hardly visible from the shore, but he shouts: "Kiiha Tikequihunga!—I'm arriving, for a fact!" The Inuit go aboard. Peary has a barrel of biscuits brought up on deck. The two or three hunters who have gone out to the ship in their kayaks bend over the barrel and begin to eat with both hands. Later, the barrel is taken ashore, and the contents thrown on the beach. Men, women and children hurl themselves on the biscuits like dogs, which amuses Peary a lot. My heart still turns cold to think of it. That scene tells very well how he considered this people—my people—who were, for all of that, devoted to him.[14]

This account of Peary by an Inuit man returns Peary to a world where there is no possible innocent reading of Peary and his "accomplishments." Within Peary's 1909 narrative, the Inuits—Uutaaq, Ukkujaaq, Iggianguaq, and Sigluk—are altogether denied a subject position. Matthew Henson, the U.S.-born, educated African American man appears a step above, yet as a man of color his accomplishments are kept clearly distinct from Peary's, and he is thus forbidden to occupy the slot of codiscoverer. When Peary claimed the elusive geographical point of the North Pole in 1909, he wrote, "The Pole was MINE . . . to be credited to me and associated with my name, generations after I ceased to be" (152). At that time he did not intend to share the credit with anyone and thus deliberately prevented any other white man from accompanying him to the pole.

The Social Relations of Discovery: Matthew Henson

Matthew Henson, who had worked for Peary for twenty-one years and had accompanied him on all seven of his Arctic expeditions, wrote about his own accomplishments at the North Pole in his 1912 book *A Negro Explorer at the North Pole: An Autobiographical Report by the Negro who Conquered the Top of the World with Admiral Robert E. Peary*. Henson's achievements earned him relative obscurity, even though Booker T. Washington, a well-known turn-of-the-century African American reformer and educator, wrote the book's introduction and inscribes Henson in a narrative of national heroism. Washington uses the same terms as Peary, however, but founders on the fact of race, a fact that perhaps is precisely what that narration and its terms omit by virtue of repressing social relations.

According to Washington, Henson was able to speak fluent Inuit (he does not mention that Peary himself was actually never able to learn the Inuit language) and to function in many other capacities, which included blacksmith, carpenter, cook, and navigator. Indeed, in Washington's account, the role of Henson extended beyond the narrowly defined place assigned to him by Peary. He indicates this by emphasizing Henson's ability to use the scientific instruments needed on the expedition—a point that Peary's narrative omits.[15] Despite the support Henson received from Washington and other members of the African American community, he did not attain the recognition from white society that was his due. Peary attained the rank of admiral, died a respected and accomplished man, and was buried in Arlington National Cemetery. Henson received a check for ninety-eight dollars from Peary as payment for a year of work. Then in 1913, Henson's achievement was met with grudging acceptance. An appeal was initiated by African American leaders in New York that resulted in President William Taft awarding Henson with a post as messenger "boy" in the U.S. Customhouse. Before his death in 1955, Henson was living on a pension of $1,020 a year and working as a parking attendant in Brooklyn.[16]

Peary drew criticism from contemporaries for even including an African American man as his sole U.S. companion to accompany him to the pole. Conservative white society refused to believe that a man of color could have the intelligence, physical endurance, motivation, and experience necessary to survive, let alone contribute to, the rigors of such a difficult scientific enterprise. In order to appease the fears of his critics, in his 1909 official account Peary minimized the significance of Henson's talents by emphasizing his role as a handyman capable of performing the tasks of several people: "Henson was part of the traveling machine . . . the taking of Henson was in the interest of economy of weight" (*NP*, 272). To explain why he chose Henson over a white man in the final party, Peary suggested that Henson "lacked as a racial inheritance the ability to lead. . . . He would not find his way back to land and it would be unfair to send him back alone" (*NP*, 273). Whether these statements were a tactic of Peary's or reflected a fundamental belief is less important than the discursive fact that this was how Peary constructed Henson's role.

Unlike Peary's official account, Henson's 1912 book foregrounds the ways in which the white men were materially and emotionally dependent on his and the Inuits' participation. For example, Henson frequently emphasizes his own position and that of the Inuits. We learn from his account that he saved Peary's life twice and that his own life was saved by one of the Inuit men that accompanied them to the pole. Indeed, Henson's insistence upon the presence of Inuit people is important in its perception and construction of the expedition. Although he concludes by emphasizing Peary's dependence on him and the Inuits, it is clear that it is a white history into which he inserts himself.

Henson's 1912 account is disappointing in the sense that he accepts his racially subordinate position as an appendage of the white man:

> Another world's accomplishment was done and finished, and as in the past, from the beginning of history, wherever the world's work was done by a white man, he had been accompanied by a colored man.[17]

Yet it is still, in this historical context, much more liberally inclined, particularly in the way it construes blackness as a presence rather than an absence. By insisting on how valuable he was to Peary, Henson sets out to redefine who and what an African American was against already-received racist stereotypes. Thus Henson's text was much more progressive than Peary's official account, which often characterized Henson as a "negro bodyservant" rather than as an African American citizen working for wages. By casting Henson not as a worker but as a "cog," Peary is able to fix Henson into a rigid social order in which differences between people are maintained by an unalterable scientific apparatus.

The representation of Henson's role within a scientific system naturalizes biological differences and sets in check any anxiety attendant on a loosening of a secure colonial economy. Perhaps the major difference between Henson's and Peary's accounts is that Henson's narrative dissociates itself from a colonial discourse of power and knowledge expressed in the guise of a discourse of science. Not only does his text refuse to promote the racism evidenced in Peary's supposedly scientific text, but it disturbs the equilibrium established by Peary's rationalist discourse that forces African American men and Inuit men to stay in their place. Instead, it reintroduces another version of scientific evolutionism slightly different from Peary's unchanging one, in which there is the idea of a path of progress. According to this position, African Americans need only develop their full cultural potential. By demonstrating their capabilities, they eventually can be accepted as equals to whites, and it is the belief in this possibility that underpins Henson's view. Indeed, Henson's narrative serves such a function. By revealing that he can not only survive but flourish in the dangerous and freezing regions of the Arctic, he establishes his mental and physical capabilities as equivalent to those of any white man, if not greater. Henson writes in his book that it was thanks to his care that Peary was able to return safely. As Henson puts it, "I often think that from the instant when the order to return [from the pole] was given until the land was again sighted, Peary was in a continual daze" (140). According to Henson's account, Peary had lost nine of his toes, and it was an ordeal for him to wear snowshoes. Thus Henson was obliged literally to carry Peary back on his sledge.

In order for Peary's official narrative to realize the generically promised adventure experience, he needs to omit reference to his infirmities and his reliance on Henson and the Eskimos. Henson's 1912 narrative presents another view, in which Peary was less autonomous. Yet both accounts concur in presenting the situation in the Arctic as one in which the moral superiority of values of reason, order, and stability reigned. It is not until 1966, over forty years after Peary was dead, that Henson, in an interview with historian Robert Fowler, upset the rigid binarism of these earlier narratives, with white standing for modernity and reason, and nonwhite standing for backwardness, irrationality, and violence:

> He [Peary] told me he wanted me to stop before I got to the pole. "I'll take one of the boys and go on from there," he said. But he had let it slip out what he was thinking.
>
> Shoot, I had been with him up there nearly twenty years. Freezing my hands, I saved his life when a musk ox tried to gore him. I helped amputate his toes. Of course I wanted to be there side by side with him. . . .

> I had my igloo built when Peary came in. I said, "I think I've overrun my mark two miles. I think I'm the first man to sit on top of the world."
>
> "What?" he said. Then, "We'll see tomorrow."
>
> Oh, he got hopping mad. No, he didn't say anything, but I could tell. I didn't know what he would do. I took all the cartridges out of my rifle before I went to sleep. Took them out and buried them in the snow. I had the only rifle in the party.
>
> After that he took Iggianguaq [one of the four Eskimos with them] and was gone about one and a half hours, long enough to take observations. He found out we'd overshot the mark.[18]

The quotation illustrates Henson's resentment toward what he perceives to be Peary's positioning of him. This led to his fear of being murdered in his sleep, as well as to disagreements, some of them hot-tempered and emotional, between Peary and Henson. Peary's scientific system of distinguishing between discrete roles was not flawless. According to Henson, the situation near the pole evoked in Peary the kind of irrational violence supposedly specific to African Americans. Henson was the one who had to hide the cartridges for the only available gun in order to ensure his own safety from Peary's violent outbursts. Peary's anger was precipitated by Henson's decision to make it to the pole ahead of Peary after learning that Peary had intended to exclude him during the final march to the pole. It was Henson who gauged distances and realized before Peary that he had made it to the pole. Peary lagged behind and thought the pole was still two miles farther. It is this alternative account of events that helped fuel yet another controversy in which Henson presents himself as not only the true discoverer of the North Pole but also cleverer than Peary by showing how he was able to outwit Peary at his own game.

By making it to the pole slightly ahead of Peary, Henson was able momentarily to subvert the codes of order and the rules embodied by white society. Accordingly, his transgressions made him subject to Peary's retaliation, which according to Henson took the following form:

> When I got back, he didn't help find me a job or anything. He tried to keep me from making that lecture tour, too. Said he would stop [prevent use of] the pictures. He didn't even shake my hand and say goodbye when we landed at Spuyten Duyvil in New York. I didn't

even have car fare. Some of the newspaper reporters had a hansom carriage. They took me home. One of them gave me five dollars. (51)

Reconstructing the North Pole Myth

In the most recent phase of reconstruction of the North Pole myth one of the leading characters in the story is S. Allen Counter, the director of the Harvard Foundation for Intercultural and Race Relations, who studied Henson as part of a project at Harvard University to trace the influence of blacks in world history. Disturbed that in 1909 a white United States refused to recognize an African American man as an equal or to grant him a share of the prize, Counter became determined that Henson would receive both the national and international recognition that he deserved:

> That becomes especially significant to me and perhaps to many others of Afro-American background because we live in an era when white heroes are constantly being made for young people. We see so little emphasis on black heroes.[19]

Counter was granted permission by the government of Denmark to travel to northwest Greenland in the summer of 1986 in part to "interview some of the Polar Eskimos who were familiar with early American explorations in the areas."[20] Counter decided to make the trip after he was told by Swedish colleagues whom he had met some years earlier at the Karolinska Nobel Institute in Stockholm, Sweden, that there were some light- and dark-skinned Inuits in Greenland whom they believed were the descendants of Matthew Henson and Robert Peary. On arrival at Moriussaq, Greenland, Counter had this story confirmed by the Inuit elders and was introduced to the sons of Henson and Peary. One year after this meeting, Counter arranged for the Henson and Peary descendants to come to the United States to meet with some of their North American relatives. Subsidized by Harvard University, whose president, Derek Bok, presented Peary's and Henson's Inuit sons with awards of recognition at the North Pole Family Reunion banquet, the group then toured East Coast places of major significance in their fathers' lives.

Counter's involvement in the North Pole Family Reunion eventually drew the attention of *National Geographic* magazine. For its hundredth anniversary issue the *Geographic* decided to include two articles on the North Pole Family Reunion, one by Counter and the other by Edward Peary Stafford, the explorer's grandson. Given that the *Geographic* had made no mention whatsoever of Henson's role in the North Pole discovery for seventy-five years, the reinscription of the image of Henson on the occasion of its hundredth anniversary is both a participation in collective amnesia of past entanglements and evidence of the institution's desire to refurbish its image at a moment of crisis.

As I mentioned in earlier chapters, the controversy over Peary's claim had continued, and much of the debate took place in the pages of *National Geographic*. Finally, the question of whether or not he reached the pole was tentatively answered in an exhaustive study conducted for the society by polar explorer Wally Herbert, who announced that Peary had missed the pole by 30 to 60 miles. *National Geographic*, troubled by the findings, decided in the end that the institution must admit that Peary made a mistake, and the magazine let Herbert publish his findings in the September 1988 issue. It was certainly more than a coincidence that this was the same issue in which the two articles appeared on Peary and Henson's Inuit offspring.

If the potential damage of Herbert's disclosure was somewhat minimized by his use of an aestheticizing discourse, as I have already argued, the celebration surrounding the Hensons' family reunion as an "ethnic success story" further diverted attention from Peary's failure. Though this was the first attention the *Geographic* had ever given to Henson, the framing of the reporting puts emphasis on Henson not as codiscoverer (now, neither of them had made it to the pole) but as "loyal and trusted companion" (428):

> Henson shared many of [Peary's] most intimate secrets. He knew all
> about Peary's sexual liaison and the children he fathered with
> Aleqasina. . . . But Henson never breathed a word of this in public.
> (428-29)

Counter's emphasis on Henson's ability to keep Peary's secret takes on a lot of weight in his narrative conclusion, for his North Pole story ends with the two men reunited after death. Believing that the "secret" between Peary and Cook helped cement the bond between the two explorers, Counter wrote to President Reagan to ask that he transfer Matthew Henson's remains to a place of honor among other heroes in Arlington National Cemetery. Counter's request was honored on April 6, 1988, when Henson's grave was moved from Woodlawn Cemetery to Arlington Cemetery. He is now reburied, in Counter's words, "beside the friend and companion with whom, 79 years earlier, he had stood at the top of the world" (429). What is excluded from the *Geographic* account, however, is that the reburial of Henson in Arlington Cemetery was a controversial affair. In 1975, Ruth Jenkins, a writer for the *Black History Week Supplement* of the *Washington Afro-American*, quotes an army official opposed to granting Henson interment rights:

> The Army has in the past opposed Mr. Henson's or any particular individual being granted interment rights in national cemeteries because that would discriminate against other civilians who may be equally deserving.[21]

Because Henson is not the only civilian to be buried at Arlington Cemetery, the army's argument that including Henson "would discriminate against other civilians who may be equally deserving" suggests that the request itself is unreasonable and informed solely by reverse discrimination. Indeed, the contrary seems to be the case, as is signified by the army's inability to acknowledge Henson as a national hero. Such resistance to accepting Henson as codiscoverer of the North Pole was typical of the continual rejection Henson received while he was alive from white society for his accomplishments. Even when his "patriotic" contribution was not completely ignored, his awards did not amount to much more than miserly tokenism.

The controversy around Henson's interment rights is excluded in Counter's revisionist account in the *Geographic*, as now the request to move Henson has been granted through presidential intervention. I would like to draw attention, however, to how Counter's narrative hesitates to emphasize race as a factor and instead privileges gender exclusively as a way to formulate Henson's national identity. This move suggests the difficulties in negotiating another discourse, tradition, or place for African Americans. Counter plays down race in favor of Henson's masculinity and his male bonding with Peary to accommodate the middle-class readership of the *Geographic*, and this works to mask the differences between the two men and the unequal power relations involved.

I will quote from Peary's writing in 1898 to explain why Counter's celebration of Henson by revealing the "secret" Arctic pasts of these two men is problematic. This text might enable Counter to claim that there was indeed a special relationship between Peary and Henson, but more significantly it reveals that the rules that made this alliance permissible were predetermined by the demands of the *Geographic*'s race and gender system. This is demonstrated by the following passage written by Peary:

> To [the Inuits] such an ordinary thing as a piece of wood was just as unattainable as is the moon to the petulant child that cries for it. Is it to be wondered at that under these circumstances a man offered me ... his wife and two children for a shining knife; and that a woman offered me everything she had for a needle?[22]

According to Peary, Inuit women functioned as objects of exchange readily available to U.S. men in return for such an ordinary object as a piece of wood. This passage makes clear that Peary in his position as colonizer was able to have whatever he desired from these women. According to his 1898 autobiography, he took full advantage of the situation and publicly made it known that he had sexual relations with a very young Inuit girl. His youthful mistress is even photographed nude in his book *Northward over the "Great Ice"* (500). Though he captions the photograph "Mother of the Seals (An Eskimo Legend)," it is the only conventional pinup image in the book in which an odalisque pose is used to indicate sexual availability. In this respect it is different from the other photographs, shot in a more documentary style, in which people are displayed as scientific rather than sexual objects. Also included in this 1898 text are explanations of how difficult it was for him to avoid being placed in provocative situations, such as the following, which he subtitles "An Embarrassing Position":

> Lee, Matt and Panikpah got away at 9:30 this morning to endeavor to get a few more deer in the last of the rapidly waning twilight. Their departure puts me in the somewhat embarrassing position of being left alone and unprotected, with five buxom and oleaginous ladies, of a race of naive children of nature, who are hampered by no feelings of false modesty or bashfulness in expressing their tender feelings. (404)

Allakasingwah, Peary's Inuit mistress and mother of his illegitimate son, Kar-ree Peary, as shown in Peary's book *Northward over the "Great Ice"*, 1:500. The original caption, "Mother of the Seals (An Eskimo Legend)," connects her with commonly held beliefs of the period that native peoples occupied an uncertain position between the human and the animal, and as such were surely not to appear as potential threats to the social hierarchy.

Peary considers white women by implication noncompliant, and thus the Inuit woman's lack of "false modesty or bashfulness" provides a rationale for why Peary considered himself under no obligation to resist such temptations. Evidently the Arctic provided a narrative space for the realization of manhood. It tested machismo and provided male readers with erotic suspense. It is significant that the focus of the two articles in the 1988 issue of the *Geographic* article on the Inuit families makes Henson retrospectively acceptable as a participant within this *Geographic* tradition, and, of course, no question arose of "recognizing" children. Counter, who is the author of one of the two *Geographic* articles, is willing to include Henson even on such problematic terms to show Peary and Henson's essential commonality. What is unsettling about this is that Counter relies on the mythos of masculine bonding as a means to define interracial solidarity. This move also works to reinforce an older colonialist discourse that sets up an opposition between the United States and the non-West. The only difference is that now African American men are asked to share in the responsibility for U.S. colonial violence. Henson is retrospectively seen as an active participant in this tradition.

Much more alarming even than Counter's rewriting of Henson is the *Geographic* article written by Peary's conservative white grandson, Edward Peary Stafford. Focusing on his trip to Greenland, where he met his Inuit kin for the first time, the article reveals that Stafford's acceptance of his "new" family is fraught with contradictions and conflicts symptomatic of his own racism. Stafford uses the language of kinship as a means to claim evidence for the unique qualities of his Eskimo descendants. As Stafford puts it, "Even after four generations the Caucasian genes can still reveal themselves with pronounced effect."[23] For Stafford, his family's white bloodline improved the Inuits' human lineage, and they were thus able to differentiate themselves from the other members of their community:

> I realized with pride that these, my relatives, were leaders of their
> people—their representatives in government, those to whom others
> came for counsel, the most skillful hunters and sled drivers (still the
> measure of a man in this high Arctic). And from this I concluded that
> the blood and the driving, enduring spirit of Robert Edwin Peary, the
> discoverer of the North Pole, live on in this wild and fiercely
> beautiful country, his "own domain," to which he devoted so much
> of his life. (421)

What is most astonishing is how Stafford concludes his narrative by erasing the achievements of his Eskimo kin within their own culture in favor of using their accomplishments to promote his own white family and culture. For Stafford, Caucasian genes play a powerful legitimizing role and provide the means by which he can distinguish his relatives from the alien "other." In this way blood and ancestry provide the illusion of a preexisting sameness and enable Stafford to accept people that under other circumstances he would dismiss as foreign and uncivilized. For here, Greenland and his Inuit relatives function merely as signifiers to demonstrate the continuing hegemony of white patriarchy and the language of kinship and blood to connote position, place, and power.

According to Stafford, Peary's ruling-class stature retains its power in the face of Herbert's claim that Peary failed to reach the pole. According to this logic, in which the figures of elite society must remain pure, there is continuing anxiety on the part of the *Geographic* to preserve Peary as an untainted hero.

The Geographic's Criterion of Greatness

To maintain the *Geographic*'s system of kinship through its pantheon of male heroes, the society commissioned yet another study, one month after the September 1988 issue appeared. This one was spurred by the remarks of Dennis Rawlins, a Baltimore astronomer who, citing Peary's own calculations, told the *Washington Post* that not only did Peary fail to reach the pole, he *knew* that he hadn't made it. Stung by the charge that their man was a fraud as well as a failure, which was printed as front-page headlines in the *Washington Post*, society president Gilbert Grosvenor called on the Navigation Foundation of Rockville, Maryland, to rescrutinize the Peary archives using purely scientific tools. Foundation scientists would reexamine the original expedition photographs, compare ocean depth soundings, and reevaluate Peary's means of navigation. The society promised that the study would leave no "unturned stones."

Significantly, the results published in December 1989 overturn the 1988 admission of Peary's failure and secure Peary's place once again among the *Geographic*'s heroes of exploration. The rhetoric of this 230-page report by Thomas Davies, which purportedly claims to be "conclusive" and "unimpeachable" in the words of the present *Geographic* editor, Gilbert Grosvenor, completely dismisses all criticism of Peary for the last seventy-five years.[24] As Davies concludes:

> We found that remarkably little new information had been introduced into the record by a succession of critical books and articles in the nearly seven decades since Peary's death.[25]

Using so-called technical proofs and modern technology to confirm the validity of Peary's word, an ideology of science, as signified by new photographic technologies, is used to make Peary an honorable figure once again. The foundation reached the following conclusion:

> By applying modern methods of close-range photogrammetry to a number of photographs that Peary identified as taken near the Pole the study determined that the position of the photographer was

essentially where Peary's final celestial observations showed him to be. We also applied this technique to a photograph made by Peary on his 1906 "farthest north" expedition and, as a check on our methodology, to a photograph of the Will Steger polar expedition taken at the Pole in May 1986. (47)

By proving that Peary was close to his asserted position, this report is able to dismiss all disagreements and to return Peary and his purported accomplishments to a state of grace exempt from tensions. Once again science comes to the rescue by establishing the truth and creating the conditions for narrative closure. Peary, the born-again hero, appears as the reasonable and controlled scientist, capable of producing authentic photographic evidence to support his claim, whereas Henson never had the benefit of photography. Thus, this new study, largely based on the evidence of Peary's photographs, remains complicitous with a discourse of empirical science that delineates a fixed set of relations in which an African American man's knowledge and more generally that of other races and nationalities continue to be subordinated to the rational and scientific knowledge of white male Americans. Such ideological preoccupations are hidden under a discourse of science that disguises its bias by having a machine rather than a person legislate the truth.

The camera as the immortal eyewitness also works to maintain a notion of order and continuity particular to the *Geographic*'s own racially marked ideology of masculinity, nationalism, and science. For what is most striking about the final report is how it accepts the original procedures and protocols used on the expedition to secure and reproduce the normative status of the white male explorer, whose superiority was unquestioned in its disguise as scientist/ explorer of the unknown. Men of color still remain excluded from the *Geographic*'s criteria of greatness. Counter's attempt to reintroduce Henson falls short in part because he defines him as dependent on Peary, rather than as autonomous. There is no such thing as reciprocal dependency in the *Geographic*'s discourse on heroism, which relies for its image on a single white hero playing the active dominant role. Significantly, the new scientific evidence used to restore Peary as a representative figure of the *Geographic*'s elite culture does not extend to Henson and thus reinforces a unitary notion of U.S. heroism as white and male. For in the recent report, Henson is still not mentioned as the codiscoverer of the North

Pole. Rather, he appears as Peary's "companion," whose account and participation remain of marginal interest to the *Geographic* writer's endorsement and validation of the figure of the white hero and his accomplishments.

4

Science and Writing:
Two Adventures of Male
Embodiment

The British were the losers in the race to the South Pole. Roald Amundsen of Norway reached the pole in 1911, one month ahead of the hapless Capt. Robert Falcon Scott. Not only did the British team fail to reach the pole first, but Scott and his four men died of hunger and cold on their way back. After completing nearly seven-eighths of the distance they encountered a blizzard and, unable to reach their food depot just 11 miles away, died in their tent from a combination of frostbite, sickness, and starvation. This was no ordinary failure, to be covered up as a national embarrassment. Rather, the tragedy of the British expedition was seized on and celebrated by the British as a national historical event. The Peary controversy was different; the uncertainty attributed to Peary's success at the North Pole was not just a straightforward case of failure, and, for reasons I will make clear, not recuperable in the way failure could be in terms of a British heroism of sacrifice.

Eight months after the Scott expedition had disappeared, a search party found the tent with the bodies of Scott and his men inside. They recovered the men's diaries, letters, and other belongings. Included among their possessions was a geological collection that included thirty pounds of rock specimens that Scott had hoped would contribute to science. Surgeon Atkinson, who buried Scott and his men, was moved by the presence of the stones:

They had stuck to these up to the very end, even when disaster stared them in the face and they knew that the specimens were so much weight added to what they had to pull.[1]

Yet the pursuit of science was only one of several goals for the British expedition; for Peary's exploit science was integrated into the expedition as a means as well as a singular goal. Peary attributed his superior abilities to management of a "traveling machine" that deployed the latest technological advances in scientific instrumentation and modes of transport. Instead, Scott's masculine performance depended simply upon the integrity and honor of being a British gentleman. In Scott's view, British minds and bodies alone were enough to display the superior capabilities of the male hero.[2]

This is why Scott is able to portray the failure of his expedition as a heroic example of British character:

Our wreck is certainly due to this sudden advent of bad weather. . . . I do not think human beings ever came through such a month as we have come through. . . . I do not regret this journey, which has shown that Englishmen can endure hardships, help one another and meet death with as great a fortitude as ever in the past.[3]

Scott's articulation of his expedition's fortitude was readily accepted by the search party, who in memory of Scott and his men chose to inscribe the following line from Tennyson's *Ulysses* on the cross marking their burial site: "To strive, to seek, to find, and not to yield."[4]

At Scott's request, his diary was given to his wife, Kathleen Scott, who with a family friend, Leonard Huxley, prepared and arranged his notes for public consumption. With funding from the British government, Scott's diary and letters were rapidly published in 1913 in London, New York, and Boston under the title: *Scott's Last Expedition: The Personal Journal of Captain R. F. Scott, R.N., C.V.O., on His Last Journey to the South Pole.*[5]

In the years following Scott's death a myth of the gentleman-hero was erected on the foundation of the letters Scott wrote to explain the causes of his expedition's misfortunes. He wrote of himself as a man who sacrificed his own life to look after the welfare of his men. His letters demonstrated his leadership qualities and his ability to face death alone. Thus a typical editorial in the London *Times* praised the failure of the Scott expedition:

Let us put out of our minds all the gossip which ... has been circulated about a race. ... The real value of the Antarctic expedition was spiritual, and therefore in the truest sense national. It is proof that in an age of depressing materialism men can still be found to face known hardship, heavy risk and even death, in pursuit of an idea. ... That is the temper of men who build empires, and while it lives among us we shall be capable of maintaining an Empire that our fathers built.[6]

Scott was able to reveal "the temper of men who build empires," thus saving Britain from the disgrace of losing to the Norwegians, by displaying the noble behavior of the "real" English gentleman. Even though Scott was not an aristocrat or a great explorer, his orderly and respectable death demonstrated the qualities of an Englishman that was born to rule.

In England, Scott's point of view was the only version of the story that was made public at the time. Although Scott makes references to the other four men who died with him in the field, their letters and diaries remained private. They were representatives of the navy, silent supporters of their commander, observers.

For many years the original diaries and letters of Scott and his men were not available to the public. Recently, some of these documents have been released. Roland Huntford, a Scandinavian historian, studied these original manuscripts and revealed in his 1979 book, *Scott and Amundsen*, the concerted effort made at the time of Scott's death by the British Admiralty to conceal unsettling facts about the Scott expedition. By comparing Scott's original diary with the published version Huntford found that

> Scott's diaries were purged of all passages detracting from a perfect
> image; particularly those revealing bitterness over Amundsen,
> criticism of his companions, and, above all, signs of incompetence.
> (*LPE*, 527)

Huntford's research revealed that Scott's diaries and letters were altered in order to turn the official version of events into something worthy of public reverence. The suggestion that Scott and his men died from scurvy was suppressed because it would have reflected on the whole conduct of the expedition. Roland Huntford provides an example of a significant excision made by a committee chaired by Kathleen Scott:

> It began with Kathleen Scott who, at her husband's request, was
> dealing with the papers. "He was the last to go," she wrote to
> Admiral Egerton, sending Scott's farewell letter to him — which
> happened to indicate otherwise. It was one of the letters found loose
> in the tent. On the back was a note in Bowers' hand, suggesting that
> Bowers may have been the last survivor, or at least casting doubts on
> Scott's claim. . . . In any case it was inconvenient evidence. It was
> suppressed and, instead, there was issued an official reconstruction
> of the closing scene in the text, contrived at the request of Kathleen
> Scott by the playwright Sir J. M. Barrie. (*LPE*, 528)

In Barrie's reconstruction of Scott's death, the social relations of the
expedition are concealed, and Scott outlasts his social inferiors:

> Wilson and Bowers died first and Captain Scott . . . thereafter . . .
> unbared his shirt and . . . with his head flung back awaited death. We
> know this because it was thus that the three were found. (*LPE*, 528)

Barrie's staged drama perpetuates an ideal of British male heroism in
which the captain, unafraid, thrusts his manly chest out in the face of
adversity and awaits death alone.

American Myths of Modernity and Masculinity

In Scott's case, failure is recuperable through writing, whereas it isn't
in terms of a U.S. evolutionist discourse of science. This cultural difference is apparent in U.S. Arctic explorer Vilhjalmur Stefansson's reaction to Scott's death in 1913:

> It has been so many years since arctic and antarctic exploration took
> any comparable toll of lives that we had come to feel fairly secure.
> After all, Peary and men like him have made exploration a science
> and with modern equipment and provision against the cold . . . there
> is not the danger that there used to be. . . .
>   But perhaps our confidence in the steadily improved equipment of
> exploring parties had grown till we have been lulled into a false
> sense of security. This disaster to the Scott party is crushing in the
> way that the wreck of the Titanic was crushing. We had grown to
> believe that traveling on the seas in a huge liner was stripped of its
> traditional perils.[7]

The myth that scientific progress had turned ocean travel and polar
exploration into risk-free activities was of fairly recent origin. The

loss of the Scott expedition was a reminder that all dangers had evidently not entirely disappeared with the recent alliance established between exploration and science. Instead, Stefansson points out that the belief in the infallibility of polar exploration and ocean travel was a sign of the new dangers that such mythologies of science engendered. Of course, the irony is that, as we shall see, Scott downplayed any alliance between scientific techniques and his expedition.

For Stefansson, the effect of the new sense of security might have proved damaging, yet he agrees that its existence was warranted. The relatively few lives lost in Arctic and Antarctic exploration in recent years showed that a significant advance had indeed been made. So much is this the case that when Stefansson is told that the failure of the Scott expedition was simply the result of a blizzard, which was considered a rather commonplace occurrence of nature, not only does he disbelieve it, but he invents a greater calamity as the cause:

> Such a tragedy could be explained only on the supposition that some great and incalculable calamity overtook the party, a calamity of the proportions of an earthquake ... an earthquake might have broken loose a huge fragment of the ice barrier ... so that they floated out to sea, but this is hard to believe. (Ibid.)

It is not surprising that Stefansson fabricates a more extreme incident in order to conform better to an ideology of modernization and progress. Evidently, a blizzard just did not count as an obstacle to Stefansson—it was too ordinary:

> No blizzard alone ever killed Captain Scott and his men. He was too experienced an explorer for that. Out on the Western prairie such a thing might be. A rancher might get caught unawares in a snowstorm, to be frozen and buried in the drifts. But in the Arctic regions? No. And certainly not when the leader was such a man as Scott, who had the finest of equipment and who knew how to guard against cold and snow. That was his business and he knew his business. (Ibid.)

Stefansson's disbelief can be attributed to a certain historical certainty of that period. Stefansson, a polar explorer himself, does not need to know Scott personally in order to assert confidence about Scott's expertise. For Stefansson, science and exploration are so intimately intertwined that it would be inconceivable that Scott as a practitioner of science would not know something as basic to the profession as how to guard against cold and snow. But did he?

For U.S. explorers such as Stefansson, who linked polar exploration to the ideology of modernization and progress, expertise was a
necessity if science was to offer as a social reality the safer world that
its apologists promised.[8] The "Peary system" that Peary described in
his book *The North Pole* ensured that his material experience measured up to the ideologically produced expectations of science:

> The source of our success was a carefully planned system,
> mathematically demonstrated. Everything that could be controlled
> was controlled, and the indeterminate factors of storms, open leads
> and accidents to men, dogs, and sledges, were taken into
> consideration in the percentage of probabilities and provided for as
> far as possible. (*NP*, 201)

The pseudoscientific Peary system provided the image under which
Peary's expedition was perceived to be infallible. The symbolics of
this system embodied a discourse that allowed no margin for error
in the practice of science. There was no room for failure, which
would be synonymous with ruin, nor was there any question that the
pole might be unwinnable. Thus, Peary's actual failure during his
seven earlier attempts to reach the North Pole could only be re-
couped once he was able finally to say that he had succeeded, and
that he was the only one to have accomplished the deed. In order to
be assured of his own victory, Peary had to make sure that his rival's
claim was discredited.

It is in this sense that U.S. science seemed to have its own set of
ethics. It did not matter that the importance given to determining the
true discoverer of the North Pole was out of proportion to any practical value attached to its attainment. Clearly, we are here dealing with
an almost purely ideological phenomenon. By the early twentieth
century almost all parts of the world were known and more or less
adequately or approximately mapped. Exploration no longer consisted of discovery but was rather a symbolic politics, a form of athletic endeavor or sport that exalted the male body and its exterior
scientific apparatus.

There was an interest in showing that a male American body as a
scientific device could dominate the most severe and inhospitable
physical environment of the globe. If attaining the North Pole was
part sporting competition for the Americans, athletic ability was not
the only thing that was being tested. For the president of the Ameri-

can Geographical Society, Gilbert Grosvenor, all of the international participants were not equally equipped for the task (see chapter 1). To Grosvenor, it was not just male physical strength that was being tested in this contest. Rather, it was the combination of physical strength and scientific ability. For Grosvenor, the United States had an advantage over the rest of the nations because it was the most scientific. In Grosvenor's narrative it is fitting that Peary, who represents the essence of U.S. identity, is depicted as a scientific manager:

> No better proof of the minute care with which every campaign was prearranged can be given than the fact that, though Peary has taken hundreds of men north with him on his various expeditions, he has brought them all back, and in good health. . . . What a contrast [Peary's] record is to the long list of [British] fatalities from disease, frost, shipwreck and starvation. (*NP*, xxxi-xxxii)

Peary is the preeminent polar explorer because he is the "most persistent and scientific" (*NP*, xxxii). "The minute care with which he prearranged every campaign" (*NP*, xxxi) enables him to overcome the flaws of early polar expeditions. For Grosvenor, the U.S. claim on the North Pole seems to make disease, famine, and other forms of human misery relics of a less scientific past. In winning the race to the North Pole, Grosvenor suggests that the Americans were able to show that the British expedition's reliance on character and determination was not enough.

It is significant that Peary, the scientific manager, represents himself as the epitome of manliness. As a figure for U.S. nationalism, the body of the U.S. polar explorer was defined by the enterprise of science in which expertise and skill rather than the inner qualities of fortitude and dignity under stress were emphasized. National moral superiority was expressed in terms of a discourse constructed by an evolutionist technology of science.

One Form of Male Sacrifice

The mythification of the Scott expedition by the British Admiralty fit within an already established tradition of British imperial heroics connected to the polar regions. Prior to the Scott expedition, male sacrifice in the polar regions served as a means to perpetuate a superior image of Britishness and British nature not motivated by self-interest.

The connection between polar exploration and a certain brand of British imperial humanism can be dated from the time of the disappearance of the earlier Franklin expedition sent out by the British navy in 1845 to discover the Northwest Passage. In order to find the lost Franklin expedition the British navy participated in a humanitarian search perhaps unparalleled in maritime history.[9] Over a period of fourteen years, forty British expeditions were sent out to look for the survivors. What most characterized these heroic rescue expeditions was a romantic notion of self-sacrifice. These men and ships were sent out to the Arctic not for material gain, but rather to save their fellow countrymen from death or to bring back their bodies. Such a display of chivalric values combined with noble sacrifice helped turn British polar explorers into romantic national figures. The metaphor of tragic self-sacrifice connoted the spirit of the nation. The virtues of British fortitude were celebrated as part of a mid-nineteenth-century romantic literary discursive tradition, as evidenced by Alfred Lord Tennyson's celebrated poem *Ulysses*, cited by Huntford:

> One equal temper of heroic hearts,
> Made weak by time and fate, but
> strong in will
> To strive, to seek, to find, and
> not to yield. (*LPE*, 117)

Tennyson's poem, originally dedicated to polar explorer Sir John Franklin, prevailed as a tradition and, fittingly, reappears in 1912 to memorialize the graves of Captain Scott and his men.

After the Napoleonic Wars, there was not much demand on the Royal Navy as a fighting force, and polar exploration became a surrogate for active service. Many who sought to escape from the monotony of peacetime enlisted. Thus arose a distinctively British naval figure, the officer who took to polar exploration as part of his ordinary career.

Sir Clements Markham, writing in 1893 on the relevance of polar exploration during his tenure as president of the Royal Geographical Society, recognized it as a nursery for our seamen, as a school for our future Nelsons [Nelson early on in his career had been a midshipman of an Arctic expedition] and as affording the best opportunities for distinction to young naval officers in times of peace.[10]

Under Markham's direction, Antarctic exploration became highly esteemed within the navy. Markham himself derived his passion for polar exploration from his early experience as a cadet in the Arctic on the second Franklin search expedition in 1850-51. He knew half a dozen languages and was a prolific writer on the history of exploration. The figure of Markham as an explorer, gentleman, and writer provides a marked contrast to Peary's image as the red-blooded, tough, competitive U.S. scientific manager:

> [Markham] seemed the embodiment of the romance of Geography; his bosom swelled, and his shirt front billowed out like the topsail of a frigate, and as his voice rose in praise of "our glorious associates," he often roused a rapturous response. (*LPE*, 126)

This description of Markham by a Royal Geographical Society official brings a potentially contradictory "softening" dimension to the image of the polar explorer. It is significant that in the case of Markham, power is ascribed in terms of sartorial and rhetorical flourish rather than physical strength or scientific expertise. To the old Arctic admiral who had not seen the ice for twenty years, the era of the 1840s and 1850s was not a blemish from a less scientific British past. Rather, he recovers the tragedies of that period as "great endeavors" and "heroic achievements." For Markham, the 1840s and 1850s was the most memorable period in polar exploration because of the countless heroic sacrifices made.

Self-sacrifice as such was valorized by the Anglican Church, according to Huntford, who cites Francis Paget, dean of Christ Church:

> Surely war, like every other form of suffering and misery, has its redeeming element in the beauty and splendor of character men, by God's grace show in it ... men rise themselves and raise others by sacrifice of self, and in war the greatness of self-sacrifice is set before us. (127)

This philosophy has its exact parallel in polar exploration, as evidenced by the following passage from Captain McClure's narrative of his 1850-54 search for Franklin:

How nobly those gallant seamen toiled ... sent to travel upon snow and ice, each with 200 pounds to drag. ... No man flinched from his work; some of the gallant fellows really died at the drag rope ... but not a murmur arose ... as the weak fell out ... there were always more than enough of volunteers to take their places. (127)

During the mid-nineteenth century the ideal of personal gallantry was seemingly an end in itself. Writing in 1893, it was this old romantic image of the polar explorer that Markham intended to keep alive:

The Polar Regions ... difficult of access ... [are] of surpassing interest and importance. Here we meet with examples of heroism and devotion which must entrance mankind for all times ... there are dangers to be encountered and difficulties to be overcome which call forth the best qualities of our race.[11]

For Markham, polar exploration was seen as a testing ground to keep alive displays of moral courage and physical bravery, as well as a place to express the superiority of the British race. In such writing, the British had very high standards of ethics when it came to themselves. They of course often applied other standards to the non-Western peoples they subjugated in their scramble for new territories and wealth. Indeed, the aesthetic side of polar exploration made for convincing imperial theater; those polar explorers who risked their lives to find the Franklin expedition became British heroes and embodied the idea of adventure but were not tarnished by the horrors of empire. These heroes of the British military caste had a less compromised image than their counterparts in the colonies, who represented quite a different personification of the British Empire. Once Adm. Sir Leopold McClintock finally discovered the remains of the Franklin expedition, an era of polar exploration had ended. So much did that period have a hold on the British imagination, however, that it was revived again in the late nineteenth century.

At the turn of the century, the tradition of polar exploration remained intact, yet now members of the middle class were able to participate in this formerly upper-class tradition (Scott himself was a member of the middle class). A whole ideological system of entitlement to rights had been erected on the assumption that certain military virtues such as courage, bravery, and manliness were innate qualities of British subjects in the Royal Navy. It now mattered less whether these men were no longer part of the upper class, for their affiliation with the Royal Navy bestowed on them the requisite authority and prestige.

In keeping with the attitudes of the Royal Navy during this period is a reconstruction of the past, or the literary attempt to transport the heroic past fictionally into the present, of which Markham's writings are one example. Only to polar explorers outside of England did such an emphasis on aesthetic literary ideals seem retrograde, especially when they were put into practice. Official British exploration had lapsed since Capt. Sir George Nares, R.N., led a naval expedition that attempted to reach the North Pole between 1875 and 1876. The expedition was a failure; the methods were outmoded, and many of the crew died of scurvy. Sir Clements Markham had repeatedly disparaged progress abroad, preferring to rely on an outmoded British method. This attitude was most evident in 1899 in his advocacy of a system of man-hauling over the use of dogs as draft animals:

> In recent times much reliance has been placed upon dogs for Arctic traveling. Yet nothing has been done with them to be compared with what men have achieved without dogs. Indeed, only one journey of considerable length has ever been performed, in the Arctic regions, with dogs—that by Mr. Peary across the inland ice of Greenland. But he would have perished without the resources of the country, and all his dogs, but one, died, owing to overwork, or were killed to feed the others. It is a very cruel system. (*LPE*, 137)

Scott had a similar moral view on dogs. This is not surprising, as Scott, like Markham, was a navy man rather than a polar explorer by profession. Scott's limited experience in the field apparently was not considered a hindrance to his ability to accomplish his goal, as experience or expertise was not necessarily highly valued in the British navy anyway. The navy, in the approving words of Adm. Sir Herbert Richmond, was "breeding amateur Naval officers" (161). As historian Roland Huntford put it:

> The study of strategy and tactics was considered almost bad form, chiefly because Nelson was erroneously believed to have triumphed at Trafalgar without a plan of battle. Most officers believed that the old hereditary idea of gallantry and dash would see them through. (161)

This faith in gentlemanly improvisation seems to point to the existence of an ideological system in which there was the belief that certain heroic virtues were innate to the British. According to this belief, it would be considered redundant to learn something that was already hereditary. From such a perspective the incorporation of new techniques readily adopted by the Americans or the Norwegians would be difficult.

Scott was not completely lacking in polar experience before his 1911 South Pole expedition. In 1905 Markham appointed him to lead the *Discovery* expedition to Antarctica. Yet his experience on this expedition did not drastically change his opinion on dogs that he had received from Markham. In his narrative *The Voyage of the Discovery* Scott also dismisses the use of skis for Antarctic exploration with the opinion "that in the Antarctic Regions there is nothing to equal the honest and customary use of one's own legs."[12]

And about the dogs, he has this to write:

> In my mind no journey ever made with dogs can approach the height of that fine conception which is realized when a party of men go forth to face hardships, dangers, and difficulties with their own unaided efforts, and by days and weeks of hard physical labor succeed in solving some problem of the great unknown. Surely in this case the conquest is more nobly and splendidly won. (1:343)

Scott is concerned above all with constructing an image of noble struggle. The polar explorer is not a scientific hero who rationally learns from his hardships and searches for advanced means to make them easier. He is someone who prefers adventure to anything else. Adversity and setback almost become morally desirable. He shuns the use of dogs because they would make the obstacle seem less formidable. Why? For Scott the basis for all this is the Englishman's ever-present willingness to prove his superiority. He does not need any assistance. He is totally self-sufficient, even in the harsh climate of Antarctica. Dogs would compromise this heroic image.

Cold Comforts

Scott's idea of masculinity put more emphasis on willpower and moral strength than did Peary's polar narratives, which depended on his control of the tools of science. Scott's particular sense of masculinity is encoded in the following letters that Scott wrote before his death in March 1912. These documents became the founding text that accounted for the rise of the Scott myth.[13]

> If this letter reaches you Bill and I will have gone out together. We are very near it now and I should like you to know how splendid he was at the end—everlastingly cheerful and ready to sacrifice himself for others, never a word of blame to me for leading him into this mess. He is not suffering, luckily, at least only minor discomforts.[14]

Scott wrote the preceding passage in a tent in Antarctica in March 1912. "This mess" that is so calmly written about, the "it" that is referred to as being "very near," is how Scott introduces the reader to the probability of his and his lieutenant Bill's (Dr. Edward Wilson) imminent deaths. This letter, however, is about Bill's death, not his own. Lying in a tent on their return from the South Pole, Scott writes a letter to Bill's wife to inform her that she is now a widow. He is reassuring. He tells her that her husband is "everlastingly cheerful." Even at the moment when he is confronted with his own death, Bill remains "splendid," "ready to sacrifice himself for others," with "never a word of blame" to Scott, who was apparently responsible. Who would blame him now, anyway, as he is dying too? But not yet, for he is still writing, consoling the grief of others. Even with death upon him Scott always thinks of others first.

In the next paragraph of Scott's letter, Bill is dead:

> His eyes have a comfortable blue look of hope and his mind is peaceful. . . . I can do no more to comfort you than to tell you that he died as he lived, a brave, true man—the best of comrades and staunchest of friends. (470)

Scott renders the last moments of Wilson's death with an aestheticizing comment: "His eyes have a comfortable blue look of hope." No other mention is made of the corpse, which marked by scurvy and frostbite must have had a rather unsightly appearance. Yet, the image of the "comfortable blue look of hope" expresses that Wilson faced death bravely, honorably. If there was any remorse or unpleasantness, Scott does not pass it on to Wilson's wife. This is what an honorable gentleman wants her to believe.

With Wilson dead or near death, Scott now writes to Mrs. Bowers, the mother of Lieutenant Henry Robertson Bowers, the other officer dying with him now in the tent:

I write when we are very near the end of our journey, and I am finishing it in company with two gallant, noble gentlemen. One of these is your son. He had come to be one of my closest and soundest friends, and I appreciate his wonderful upright nature, his ability and energy. As the troubles have thickened his dauntless spirit ever shone brighter and he has remained cheerful, hopeful, and indomitable to the end. (470)

This letter, like the earlier one, seems chiefly motivated by an impulse to reveal nothing concrete about the reality of Lieutenant Bowers's death. Scott is describing not the event of Bowers's death but an aesthetic representation. The narrative culminates with an image of Bowers not as a flesh-and-blood man but as a "dauntless spirit."

Scott concludes his letter by connecting the idealized image of Bowers's "dauntless spirit" to another mythical site of unity and harmony—the respectable English bourgeois family. Bowers's last memories of happiness, his ability to remain "splendidly hopeful to the end," are due to his "happy home." In the final sentences of Scott's letter the dying Bowers and his family exist in a mutually authorizing relationship:

To the end he has talked of you and his sisters. One sees what a happy home he must have had and perhaps it is well to look back on nothing but happiness. He remains unselfish, self-reliant and splendidly hopeful to the end, believing in God's mercy to you. (471)

By establishing a tie between Bowers's noble death in Antarctica and the familial home in England, Scott connects the two remote places, Antarctica and England. Yet what is striking is how he erases the harsh conditions of Antarctica by portraying Bowers's death in such a psychically undisturbing way that it appears as if he had died a natural death in England.

Scott writes both these letters in the first person, yet within his narrative he seems to exist as the detached third person. Although Scott is at the scene of the event, he appears to be far away. His attention to formal literary conventions in his letters suggests that Scott is not freezing and starving to death in a tent in Antarctica but rather sitting at his desk somewhere in a comfortable London flat.

Scott avoids altogether any passing references to frozen bodies or to death in Antarctica. He refers to the harshness of the situation in only the most perfunctory way: "Excuse writing—it is -40 and has been nigh for a month." Instead, Scott populates the scene with images and voices from England through the writing of numerous letters to the families of his men, to his own family and friends, and to his superior officers in the Admiralty. Also, by employing a style that is distancing and artificially associative, he manages to avoid any direct reference to the horror of the situation at hand. Moreover, his use of clipped naval expressions such as "we are pegging out in a comfortless spot," "we have shipped up," "a close shave," and "shot our bolt" expresses that his impending death and the death of his men have left his dignity and bearing intact in the community of a courageous male crew.

Through Scott's letters, Antarctica is a theater in which a performance by British naval officers can be seen from the privileged standpoint of England.[15] Thus, Antarctica is textualized; it becomes a discursive space in which intrepid British naval officers can prove that they can still die as gentlemen. Never deviating from their routine, they face death as they did life—unruffled, certain of themselves, and dignified. There are no last minute attempts to save themselves. All in all, the fiction of Scott's narrative construction has a predictably tidy end, with everything properly explained by Scott, down to an account of his men's final dying words.

Nothing could better imply the superiority of the men of the British race than Scott's staunch adherence to principle, his national consciousness, and his sense of responsibility to the nation as a whole. The absence of cowardliness showed that he and his men died nobly, without shame. Even under the most horrible of circumstances they were able to appear unassailable in themselves (heroic, brave), capable of dying honorably even from the most ignoble of deaths. If Scott and his men were unable to perform a deed worthy of heroes, at least they were able to die in heroic fashion.[16]

All Body, No Technique

There are two men of the polar party—Evans and Oates—whose mothers and wives Scott didn't bother writing letters to. These men were already dead. Evans died one month earlier; Oates died soon afterward. The disagreements between Scott, Oates, and Evans, reported in Roland Huntford's book *Scott and Amundsen*, make it clear that these men before they died were critical of Scott's leadership abilities.[17] According to Huntford, Evans was especially demoralized by the failure of the expedition to get to the South Pole first. It was intolerable to him that the Norwegian team led by Amundsen beat them. His bitterness seems to derive from a class position different from Scott's. Evans was depending on the financial security and promotion such a feat would have brought. For him, attaining the pole without the reward of priority meant failure and ruin. According to Huntford, who had privileged access to Oates's diary, Oates was more of a manager. He felt betrayed by Scott's incompetent leadership. The most blatant example of this, according to Huntford, was when Scott unexpectedly decided to take five men with him to the pole rather than four. This change of mind threw the whole intricate organization of his expedition dangerously out of joint. Everything was arranged for four-man units: tents, gear, cookers, fuel, and the depots of food along the route. Although Oates, according to Huntford, saw the foolishness of Scott's capricious decision, he remained silent and wrote self-disparagingly in his diary about his own inability to intervene.

Scott, in his letters to his friends and family, maintains an understanding, benevolent attitude toward Evans and Oates. He represents Evans, who apparently became insane from scurvy before he died,[18] as one of the "sick" that he and his men stuck to until the end. He honors Oates, who committed suicide, for noble self-sacrifice. This not only makes Oates's suicide less dishonorable but makes it fit better into the image of fraternity that Scott constructs in his letters.

Scott imagines the navy to be a community, regardless of the actual inequality that may have prevailed. When Scott writes to Vice Adm. Sir Francis Charles Bridgeman, "We could have come through had we neglected the sick," he displays his willingness to sacrifice his own life, even for men of a lower rank, to perpetuate an image of fraternity based on duty and on hierarchical comradeship.[19]

Scott became an established British tradition during World War I, according to Huntford, who cites the following 1916 entry from a British newspaper:

> After a notable bout of disaster, he [Scott] had given his countrymen an example of endurance. . . . We have so many heroes among us

now, so many Scotts ... holding sacrifice above gain [and] we begin
to understand what a splendor arises from the bloody fields ... of
Flanders ... and Gallipoli. (*LPE*, 528)

The Scott tradition lingered on. Writing in 1959, British historian L. P.
Kirwan recounts the familiar storyline:

> Such are the bare facts of Scott's approach to the Pole. The rest of the
> story, the exhausting march across the plateau, manhauling all the
> way; the sight of Amundsen's black flag tied to a sledge-bearer at the
> Pole; the tell-tale marks of sledge tracks, skis, dogs' paws; the death
> of Evans, Oates' self-sacrifice, the utter dejection and tragic end of the
> homeward journey are part of our heritage.[20]

Churches and schools became the public sites for passing down the
Scott tradition to future generations.

What is striking is the construction of masculinity immortalized
through the Scott letters. Through the act of writing, a nationalist
myth was established in which writing itself becomes a means to my-
thologize an ideology of masculinity in which paradoxically the male
body is ignored. Or rather, the male body's performance becomes
the means by which a moral theater is constructed, in which the
body ultimately disappears. The gendered, physical body is replaced
by moral character, which provides the foundation on which masculinity becomes heroicized. The exterior world also loses its concrete-
ness in Scott's account. An expedition to the South Pole expresses an
exploration into British character. It does not serve as a means to iso-
late and exalt a virile and potent male body, as Peary's account suggests. The worst possible ending for Scott would be not death but a
failure in moral resolve. Thus, in the narrative of national character,
Scott and his men literally sacrifice their bodies and exemplify self-
less courage in order to legitimize their claim to rule.

Gender and Narrative Form

Writing had a different role in the construction of the Scott myth and
in the U.S. stories on polar exploration. I have pointed out how in
Britain, the Scott story is, from beginning to end, enmeshed in writing. Its transcending aspect is expressed by Scott's encounter with

death and miraculous resurrection through his diary and letters. Writing offers a form of presence in absence, a means of salvation by which disorder, meaninglessness, and death are overcome.

In the case of Scott's story, there is also an importance given to the rhetoric of writing well, rather than truly or accurately. The recruitment of a British playwright by Scott's wife to rewrite his diaries hints at a whole literary tradition at work here from the very beginning. In Scott's letters the authority created is anchored to a large extent in subjective experience as mediated and authorized by a literary style. By writing that "we could have come through had we neglected the sick," Scott claims that he exposed himself and his men to additional dangers and personal sacrifices and connects his actions to a higher national mission as defined by the metaphor of tragic self-sacrifice, which belongs to romantic literary discursive conventions.[21] On the other hand, in contrast to the British, the Americans are trying to produce a narrative that is part of a scientific tradition. There is a larger emphasis on exteriority. Performance and achievement matter most. The scientific ideal calls for professional detachment and scientific proofs. The rhetoric of science does not allow for subjectivity except in the form of "genius," or for a sacrifice for a collective identity.

The two narratives, however, have more in common than one might expect from such different genres. In both, authority resides in the effacement of the speaking and experiencing subject. The different genres chosen suited the particular imperial ideologies that each writer was promoting.[22] Scott's story was coded within the static and timeless genre of tragedy, expressing the desire of England to maintain its dominion of the past into the present. The Americans, instead, glorified a progressive scientific ideology that looked more to the future but also wanted immortality. Still, while Scott's subjectivity is understood and constituted in terms of literary ideals, Peary's is defined by scientific objectives. While tragedy is acceptable within the parameters of the literary, there is no place for it within Peary's or Stefansson's scientific discourse. It would be considered simply a catastrophic error of judgment.

Peary and Stefansson anchored the authority of their discourse under the banner of science and progress. They also apportioned different qualities—those of nature-to-be-conquered—to the scene of the poles. Scott instead adopted literary conventions of the sublime to explain his own tragic situation to a British public. In Scott's letters, the landscape of Antarctica is vast, wild, tumultuous, and awful (suggestive of infinity). The blizzard that Scott encounters and blames for the tragedy represents a vast, chaotic, and frightful aspect of nature and is associated with pain and feelings of terror. England, which Scott represents, in contrast represents all that is good, or-dered, and agreeable.

The point of departure for Peary and Stefansson is totally different, for their narrative is organized around the conquest of nature. Not only do they find positive values for those aspects of the landscape that Scott sees as vast, terrifying, and misproportioned, but they even feel at home there. This homeliness, however, is expressed in terms of some extreme scientific alienation from the environment. In Ste-fansson's discourse Antarctica no longer represents the unknown, as science has already conquered it and made it familiar. "Mankind" now dominates over nature. There are no longer any parts of the globe that can pose a threat. Within such an ideology of modernity and progress, there is no place for a tragic hero such as Scott. Neither can Antarctica provide the accompanying stage by which "man" can obtain glory by recognizing his own limits. For at this stage in the U.S. discourse of progress, science and technology have abolished these limits.

British and American Media Traditions

In the wake of *Scott and Amundsen*, there was a British television series titled "The Last Place on Earth" based on Huntford's book.[23] The seven-and-a-half-hour epic was one of British television's most ambitious and costly drama series. The series presented Scott as an arrogant and amateurish leader who brought death on himself and his team by inadequate planning and by incompetence before and during the expedition. Such a portrait was inevitably controversial and was condemned by Dr. John Hemming, director of the Royal Geographical Society:

> I am very, very disappointed. The acting is superb and the whole presentation is excellent but the length to which it goes to find elements of anti-British bias and anti-Scott bias is just ludicrous. The way in which it is hysterically anti-patriotic is ridiculous.[24]

Roland Huntford, formerly the Scandinavian correspondent of the *Observer*, spent five years researching *Scott and Amundsen*. On its publication in 1979, the book created considerable controversy. The film rights were purchased by British Central Television's series executive producer, Robert Buckler, who approached Trevor Griffith to write the screenplay. Griffith was distinguished as a political playwright and by his commitment to the more popularly accessible forms of television and the cinema. For Griffith, much of the story's contemporary relevance was that it carried fundamental lessons for Britain in the 1980s:

> We are living with a government that constantly exhorts us to return
> to the great Imperial traditions of this nation, and to embrace not just
> the rhetoric but the practices of the Victorians and the Edwardians.
> So the series looks at the characteristics of the age, at the class
> differences and at the age of nationalism. (12)

Griffith's reworking of the Scott story illuminates what is at stake in "living with a government that constantly exhorts us to return to the great Imperial traditions." For Griffith, "The Last Place on Earth" provided an allegory for the Thatcher government and its nostalgic relation with the class-based values, hierarchic structures, and "news management" of the Victorian age:

> At a time when news management has reached such appalling levels
> as in the reporting of the Falklands, the Korean Airlines disaster and
> the invasion of Grenada, it seems important to look at how a myth of
> glorious and heroic failure was constructed in that way. (12)

The Thatcher government regained popularity after the Falklands/Malvinas War, a result of the rise of nationalist sentiments. The enthusiasm for the Scott story similarly relied on a reworking of patriotic sentiments. As I demonstrated earlier, the Scott myth has enjoyed especial power, for it can function well in a later period of real decline of empire (World War I to the present), or in an era imbued with a sense of imminent decline, as was the case at the time of Scott's death. Scott's military discipline and loyalty stood out as a timeless example of a universal British tradition that would put an end to anxieties about national weakness. Andy Metcalf points out how this process was exemplified in the conduct and aftermath of the Falklands War:

A war fought at considerable cost, with significant casualties, for a few bleak, scarcely populated islands with a lot of sheep, was enough to reverse the Conservative Party's slump in popularity and win them the 1983 general election. This was no mean feat—and it was largely due to the symbolic meanings attached to going to war. Churchillian phrases dripped from the mouths of the "War Cabinet," as a sordid xenophobic enterprise was transformed into a paean to manhood, a celebration of the phallus draped in the Union Jack. Resurgent nationalism and a refurbished manhood were fused into one as the ships left port, the jets screamed overhead, and wives and sweethearts cried and waved goodbye. Everyone was in their place. We'd seen the movie a hundred times: Now it was time for the real thing.[25]

The aftermath both of Scott's tragedy and of the Falklands War had remarkable power. In Britain, where the Labour party and the Left still have some control of the public media, however, there is a greater possibility of popular critique of national policies, as evidenced by "The Last Place on Earth." In contrast, the debate around Peary in the media has remained privatized—within the control of the National Geographic Society and its magazine—and thus the critiques of Peary have not touched on wider political issues but instead have remained narrowly focused on establishing or disputing the accuracy of Peary's claim to the North Pole.

Despite the confinement of the North Pole controversy to a narrowly technicist realm of ideas, why is it that this debate still prevails today? Why can't it be resolved by concluding that the pole was simply unwinnable? These questions can only be explained in terms of understanding that the North Pole was also perceived as a mythologized image of empire at the early part of the twentieth century. In this respect, the controversy around the conquest of the North Pole can be seen as an allegory for more recent symbols of U.S. imperial mythography, such as the Vietnam War and more recently the Persian Gulf War. Hannah Arendt describes how the U.S. government masked a host of contradictions in order that the historical event match the fantasy in Vietnam:

> The Vietnam War was exclusively guided by the needs of a superpower to create for itself an image which would convince the world that it was, indeed, the mightiest power on earth. Image making as global policy was something new in the huge arsenal of human follies recorded in history. . . . [Image making] was permitted

to proliferate throughout the ranks of all governmental services, military and civilian—the phony body counts of the search and destroy missions, the doctored after-damage reports of the air force, the constant progress reports to Washington.[26]

Like the North Pole, Vietnam was a male testing ground. In both events there was shame attached to losing and thus forgoing the opportunity to demonstrate one's manhood. The denial of failure establishes a continuity between these two national events. J. Hoberman describes in his article "Vietnam: The Remake" how the traumatic experience of the loss of the Vietnam War was rewritten by Hollywood cinema:

> Vietnam offered no great battles and no clearly defined enemy. Its casualties included our longstanding sense of national innocence and masculine identity, not to mention the broad national consensus that had defined American foreign policy. This has made the war particularly difficult to represent: inherently polarizing and depressing, with a built-in unhappy ending, it both broke the conventions of civilized warfare and the basic rules of Hollywood entertainment. It was the last picture show.
>
> The impossible longing for a satisfactory conclusion tempts each Viet film to sell itself as definitive. It is precisely that bummer of a finale . . . that has left us with a compulsion to remake, if not history, then at least the movie. (195)

The rewriting of Vietnam by Hollywood makes U.S. soldiers appear as victims of superiors, bureaucrats, and communists. Soldiers crack up, are cowardly, and fuck up (kill civilians). Yet Vietnam heroism exists both in spite of and against U.S. government policy.

Setting Things Aright: Technology, the Gulf War, and Peary

The denial of failure was enacted not only in Hollywood stage sets but also in the Persian Gulf region. After the so-called allied victory, the legacy of the Vietnam War was cited as a disease that had been overcome.[27] On March 3, 1991, President George Bush declared, "We have kicked the Vietnam Syndrome."[28] Bush had promised that the Persian Gulf War would be different—a neater package and easier to understand, with clear closure and an unambiguous resolution. Just as Peary's complex story has been rewritten by the *Geo-*

graphic with a happy ending reinstating Peary as an uncontroversial U.S. hero, so too has the Persian Gulf "victory" restored good feelings about a previously denigrated United States in decline. And, in both cases, the discursive logic of this favorable outcome turns on technology as unchallengeable or seemingly undefeatable. *Gender on Ice* has been my attempt to explain the interconnections between the multiple narratives of national identity, scientific progress, modernity, and masculinity across the national cultures of the United States and the United Kingdom. Once one of these discourses is invoked, the others are immediately brought into play. In this sense the Falklands and Malvinas, Vietnam, and Persian Gulf narratives parallel those of both Scott and Peary.

During the Gulf War advanced weaponry was brought in to restore the old national narratives of success; in a similar way, new high-tech photographic process presumably solved the problem of Peary's inaccuracy at the North Pole. The seamless performance of technology was more important for the Americans, who unlike the British never showed in the media a precision weapon that missed.[29] For the Americans, winning the Gulf War was inextricably tied to the myth of technological prowess embodied in high-tech electronic weaponry (Stealth fighters, spy satellites, Patriot missiles, and Tomahawk cruise missiles that were dependent on "perfect" maps drawn of Iraqi territory and terrain).

Moreover, the war was programmed in terms of its media presentation, and in various ways failure was written out of the narrative from the beginning. The televisual apparatus in general, and TV news in particular, joined forces with the military to narrate the event in a way that would sanitize and prettify the war in order to associate it with a pre-Vietnam vision of U.S. innocence and righteous virtue. Following this logic it is not surprising that the Gulf War was scripted as a replay of World War II with its reassuring overtones of justice, democracy, and victory rather than of Vietnam with which it had more in common. In these presentations, the performance of so-called smart technology was thought to be so infallible that in the earliest hours of the bombing, CNN's Pentagon reporter, Wolff Blitzer, claimed that the 150,000-man Republican Guard had been crippled or destroyed by air strikes alone.

Such exaggerated claims for the efficacy of technological weaponry kept alive the belief, which was an inextricable part of the Peary narrative, that technology was unbeatable and that the structure of operations was somehow both bloodless and unerring. In contrast to Vietnam, which could not be figured as a clean war, the Persian Gulf War was represented as strangely antiseptic and disembodied, as media coverage focused on the performance of U.S. smart bombs and surgically precise air attacks.[30] Reportage focused on identifying viewers with the pilots doing the bombing rather than with those civilians being bombed (the elision of images of Iraqi deaths or casualties). Brown bodies in general were shown as having little presence to Americans except as mere numbers. The Persian Gulf War was far more successful in rendering abstract and erasing enemy brown bodies than was the Vietnam War, where their suffering and death were made all too palpable on home television. It was not until weeks afterward that a Western audience heard that 70 percent of the 88,500 tons of bombs dropped on Iraq missed their targets and hit thousands of civilians instead.[31]

The righteous modern violence on behalf of the Western international community was contrasted to the primitive, barbaric violence of Saddam Hussein's forces.[32] Where Saddam Hussein and the Iraqis were represented as irrational beings with an uncontrollable sexual drive (Iraq was shown as having "raped" Kuwait, which required massive if "surgical" retaliation), Bush and the Western soldiers were identified as representative of heroic Western masculinity, now cured of previous "impotence" suffered in Vietnam.

The reactive Rambo style of Western masculinity tended to dominate the media's account of the war. One thinks of Colin Powell's "cut it off and kill it" or Schwarzkopf's promise to "kick butt" or the reports of pilots watching porn videos before ejaculating their bombs over Iraq.[33] Yet despite the overblown masculinist rhetoric, this imagery did not seem anything more than a feeble attempt to remasculinize or regender social relations in an age in which heroism had less to do with the body and more to do with delegating work and manipulating electronic data. Take, for example, the *San Francisco Chronicle* poster that appeared during the Gulf War with the caption "A lot can happen between 9 & 5," featuring a before-and-after shot of Sylvester Stallone as Rambo, bare-chested and armed to the teeth, and of a fully clad rotund General Schwartzkopf as the top Allied manager.

Only two years after the war, it was significant that the war as experience and symbol was no longer being evoked, despite the fact that the media engineered a broad consensus in favor of the war. The "victory" in the Persian Gulf had largely unraveled, and the war was seen as having much more of an ambiguous or murky ending. Saddam was still in power, and the claims of military technological know-how were seen as vastly overrated by the Pentagon itself.[34] Rather than exulting over their country's military victory in the Persian Gulf, Americans worried about corrupt politicians, the recession, and increasing budget cuts on domestic programs. The implementation of an older narrative that was supposed to supplant the Vietnam syndrome (the narrative of failure) seems not to work well in a radically changed and uncertain post-cold war context. There was a strong feeling that things would never be the same again, and one wonders how viable the ideological narrative of scientific progress that has framed the discourses of the *National Geographic* and the story of the Persian Gulf War will be in the future. What new narratives of Americanism and masculinism will replace them? Will new stories be produced that do not rely solely on technology as the transcending foundation of a gender- and race-based Americanism?

Notes

INTRODUCTION

1. Joseph Conrad, *Heart of Darkness* (New York: Norton, 1963), 8.

2. Christopher Miller, *Blank Darkness: Africanist Discourse in French* (Chicago: University of Chicago Press, 1985), 5-6.

3. My discussion draws significantly on Edward Said's *Orientalism* (New York: Vintage, 1979). I also profited from Christopher Miller's *Blank Darkness*, as well as the following: Benedict Anderson's *Imagined Communities: Reflections on the Origin and Spread of Nationalism* (London: Verso, 1985) and James Clifford's *Predicament of Culture* (Cambridge: Harvard University Press, 1988). Also central was the work of feminists that relates issues of feminist theory to critiques of colonial discourses and nationalisms. In particular see Donna Haraway, *Primate Visions: Gender, Race, and Nature in the World of Modern Science* (New York: Routledge, 1989); Deborah Gordon, ed., Special Issue on Feminism and the Critique of Colonial Discourse, *Inscriptions*, nos. 3/4 (1988); Andrew Parker, Mary Russo, Doris Sommer, and Patricia Yaeger, eds., *Nationalisms and Sexualities* (New York: Routledge, 1992); Anne McClintock, " 'No Longer in a Future Heaven': Women and Nationalism in South Africa," *Transition* 51 (1991); and Chandra Talpade Mohanty, Ann Russo, and Lourdes Torres, eds., *Third World Women and the Politics of Feminism* (Bloomington: Indiana University Press, 1991).

4. Robert Peary, "The Value of Arctic Exploration." *National Geographic*, December 1903, 436.

5. For a fine analysis of U.S. empire-building activities in Central America and the Caribbean see George Black, *Good Neighbor: How the United States Wrote the History of Central America and the Caribbean* (New York: Pantheon, 1988), 1-30.

6. Evelyn Fox Keller, "Making Gender Visible in the Pursuit of Nature's Secrets," in Teresa de Lauretis, ed., *Feminist Studies / Critical Studies* (Bloomington: Indiana University Press, 1986), 68.

7. Frank Norris, *A Man's Woman* (New York: Grosset & Dunlap, 1899), 242.

8. In his essay "Geography and Some Explorers," Joseph Conrad claimed to have been inspired as a writer by the diary of a polar explorer. See *National Geographic*, March 1929, 239-74.

9. Thanks to Rob Nixon for his helpful advice on Virginia Woolf's *To the Lighthouse* and for reading earlier drafts of this introduction.

10. Virginia Woolf, *To the Lighthouse* (San Diego, Calif.: Harcourt Brace Jovanovich, 1955), 53-55.

11. Ibid., 55.

12. In particular see Judith Walkowitz, *Prostitution and Victorian Society: Women, Class and the State* (Cambridge: Cambridge University Press, 1980); Jeffrey Weeks, *Sex, Politics and Society: The Regulation of Sexuality Since 1800* (London: Longman, 1981).

13. For an account of the challenges feminist theory has posed to male conceptions of objectivity, see Evelyn Fox Keller, *Reflections on Gender and Science* (New Haven, Conn.: Yale University Press, 1985); Sandra Harding, *The Science Question in Feminism* (Ithaca, N.Y.: Cornell University Press, 1986). For an examination of feminist theory and antiessentialism see Elizabeth Grosz, "Sexual Difference and the Problem of Essentialism," *Inscriptions*, no. 5 (1989): 86-101; Gayatri Spivak, "Criticism, Feminism, and the Institution," *Thesis Eleven*, nos. 10/11, 1984/5.

14. Monique Wittig, "One Is Not Born a Woman," *Feminist Issues*, Winter 1981, nos. 1/2, 47-54.

15. Gayle Rubin, "The Traffic in Women: Notes on the Political Economy of Sex," in Rayna Rapp Reiter, ed., *Toward an Anthropology of Women* (New York: Monthly Review, 1975), 157-210.

16. The political positions of feminists of color were first made available in the following books: Cherrie Moraga and Gloria Anzaldúa, eds., *This Bridge Called My Back: Writings by Radical Women of Color* (New York: Persephone, 1981); Gloria Hull, Patricia Bell Scott, and Barbara Smith, eds., *All the Women Are White, All the Blacks Are Men, but Some of Us Are Brave* (New York: Feminist Press Anthology, 1982). Also see Audre Lorde, "The Master's Tools Will Never Dismantle the Master's House," in *Sister Outsider* (New York: Crossing, 1984); Gloria Anzaldúa, ed., *Borderlands, La Frontera: The New Mestiza* (San Francisco: Spinsters/Aunt Lute, 1987); and the more recent book edited by Gloria Anzaldúa, *Making Face, Making Soul: Haciendo Caras* (San Francisco: Aunt Lute, 1990).

17. bell hooks, *Feminist Theory: From Margin to Center* (Boston: South End, 1984), 43-44.

18. For approaches to masculinities and nationalisms that break with paradigms that treat each as discrete and autonomous, see Parker et al., *Nationalisms and Sexualities*. For more on this question as well as specifically feminist approaches to masculinities, see *Camera Obscura* 17/18 (1988), Constance Penley and Sharon Willis, eds., Special issues on Male Trouble; Eve Kosofsky Sedgwick, *Between Men: English Literature and Male Homosocial Desire* (New York: Columbia University Press, 1985); Cynthia Enloe, *Making Feminist Sense of International Politics: Bananas, Beaches and Bases* (Berkeley: University of California Press, 1989); Susan Jeffords, *The Remasculinization of America: Gender and the Vietnam War* (Bloomington: Indiana University Press, 1989); and Haraway, *Primate Visions*.

19. See Arthur Brittan, *Masculinity and Power* (London: Basil Blackwell, 1989); Kobena Mercer, "Recoding Narratives of Race and Nation," *Independent*, January/

February 1989, 19-26; Andy Metcalf and Martin Humphries, eds., *The Sexuality of Men* (London: Pluto, 1985); J. H. Pleck, *The Myth of Masculinity* (Cambridge, Mass.: MIT Press, 1981); Lynne Segal, *Slow Motion: Changing Masculinities, Changing Men* (New Brunswick, N.J.: Rutgers University Press, 1990); Klaus Theweleit, *Male Fantasies*, vols. 1 & 2 (Minneapolis: University of Minnesota Press, 1987).

20. Brittan, *Masculinity and Power*, 4.

21. Anderson, *Imagined Communities*; Paul Gilroy, *There Ain't No Black in the Union Jack: The Cultural Politics of Race and Nation* (London: Hutchinson, 1987); George Mosse, *Nationalism and Sexuality: Middle-Class Morality and Sexual Norms in Modern Europe* (Madison: University of Wisconsin Press, 1985).

22. Thomas D. Davies, *Robert E. Peary at the North Pole* (Rockville, Md.: Foundation for the Promotion of the Art of Navigation, 1989).

1. NATIONALISM ON ICE

Immediately subsequent references to a source cited in the notes will be indicated in the text by page numbers in parentheses.

1. C. D. B. Bryan, *The National Geographic Society: 100 Years of Adventure and Discovery* (New York: Abrams, 1987), 65. Bryan's book is an official celebratory history of the National Geographic Society written to commemorate the society's hundredth anniversary.

2. Michel Foucault, "What Is an Author" in Joseph V. Harari, ed., *Perspectives in Post-Structuralist Criticism* (Ithaca, N.Y.: Cornell University Press, 1979), 27-50.

3. For a detailed historical analysis of the National Geographic Society during its earliest years, see Phillip J. Pauley, "The World and All That Is in It: The National Geographic Society, 1888-1918," *American Quarterly* 31, no. 4 (Fall 1979). For a general American historical overview of this period see David Healey, *US Expansionism: The Imperialist Urge in the 1890s* (Madison: University of Wisconsin Press, 1970), 99-112.

4. Peary was a member of the society from its beginnings in 1888. He was elected an honorary member in 1903; the Hubbard Gold Medal was presented to him on behalf of the society by President Roosevelt in 1906; and in 1909 a Special Gold Medal celebrating the discovery of the North Pole was made in his honor and presented to him by the society. When Peary retired from active exploration he was elected to National Geographic's Board of Trustees.

5. See the following government documents: *Congressional Record*, 61st Cong., 3d sess., 46, pt. 3, and 64th Cong., 1st sess., 1911, 53, pts. 13 and 14. For an account of the 1911 congressional committee findings see Wally Herbert, *The Noose of Laurels: Robert E. Peary and the Race to the North Pole* (New York: Atheneum, 1989), 339-53, and Frederick J. Pohl's introduction in Frederick A. Cook, *Return from the Pole* (New York: Pellegrini & Cudahy, 1951), 33-34. This work will be cited in the text as *RP*. For further historical information on the Peary-Cook controversy, also see Pierre Berton, *The Arctic Grail: The Quest for the North West Passage and the North Pole, 1818-1909* (New York: Viking, 1988), 586-612.

6. For a detailed critical discussion of Peary's expedition and the conflict of interest of the National Geographic Society, see Dennis Rawlins, *Peary at the North Pole: Fact or Fiction?* (Washington, D.C.: Robert Luce, 1973).

7. Bryan, *100 Years*, 66.

8. Wally Herbert, "Did Peary Reach the Pole?" *National Geographic*, September 1988, 387-413. The argument in this article is expanded on in Wally Herbert, *The Noose of Laurels: Robert E. Peary and the Race to the North Pole* (London: Hodder & Stroughton, 1989).

9. Thomas D. Davies, "New Evidence Places Peary at the Pole," *National Geographic*, January 1990, 46-61.

10. Robert E. Peary, *The North Pole: Its Discovery in 1909 under the Auspices of the Peary Arctic Club* (New York: Stokes, 1910; Mineola, N.Y.: Dover, 1986), xxxvii. This work will be cited in the text as *NP*.

11. In 1827, the British offered a reward for the first European man to reach the North Pole. Attempts to reach the pole after 1882, however, were made by explorers of nations of less international significance than Britain: Italy, Sweden, Norway, and the United States.

12. Although some Eskimos prefer today to be known as Inuit, I have decided to use the term Eskimo throughout this chapter, consistent with the usage in the historical sources used and quoted.

13. Frederick A. Cook, *My Attainment of the Pole: Being the Record of the Expedition that First Reached the Boreal Center 1907-1909* (New York: Kennerly, 1913), 8-9.

14. See: U.S. Congressional Hearing Supplement, House Committee on Naval Affairs, "Statement of Captain Robert E. Peary, United States Navy," January 7, 1911, 23-39.

15. Originally appeared in "Whitney Believes Both Peary and Cook Reached the North Pole," *Boston Herald*, September 29, 1909.

16. On the crisis of white manhood at the turn of the century see Donna Haraway, "Teddy Bear Patriarchy: Taxidermy in the Garden of Eden, New York City, 1908-1936," in *Primate Visions: Gender, Race, and Nature in the World of Modern Science* (New York: Routledge, 1989), 26-58; Cynthia Enloe, *Making Feminist Sense of International Politics: Bananas, Beaches and Bases* (Berkeley: University of California Press, 1989); Roderick Nash, *Wilderness and the American Mind*, 3d ed. (New Haven, Conn.: Yale University Press, 1982); Mark Selzer, "The Love Master," in Joseph A. Boone and Michael Cadden, eds., *Engendering Men: The Question of Male Feminist Criticism* (New York: Routledge, 1990), 140-58; and Ronald Takaki, *Iron Cages: Race and Culture in Nineteenth Century America* (New York: Knopf, 1979).

17. Theodore Roosevelt, "The Strenuous Life," in *The Works of Theodore Roosevelt* (New York: Scribner, 1924-26), 15:267, 271.

18. Selzer, "The Love Master," 140; Originally appeared in Ernest Thompson Seton, *Boy Scouts of America: A Handbook of Woodcraft, Scouting and Life-Craft* (New York: Doubleday, 1910), xi. On Baden Powell and the Boy Scout Movement see Allen Warren, "Citizens of the Empire: Baden Powell, Scouts and Guides, and an Imperial Ideal," in John M. Mackenzie, ed., *Imperialism and Popular Culture* (Manchester: Manchester University Press, 1986), 232-56.

19. On eugenics, sexuality, birth control, and immigration, see Linda Gordon, *Women's Body, Women's Right: A Social History of Birth Control in America* (New York: Viking, 1976); Rosalind Rosenberg, *Beyond Separate Spheres: Intellectual Roots of Modern Feminism* (New Haven, Conn.: Yale University Press, 1982).

20. For an extended discussion of masculinity as represented in the historical novels of the 1890s, see Amy Kaplan, "Romancing the Empire: The Embodiment of American Masculinity in the Popular Historical Novel of the 1890s," in *American Literary History* 2, no. 4 (Winter 1990): 659-90.

21. Roosevelt, "The Strenuous Life," 15:267.

22. The white women that appear in the genre are mostly the wives of the explorers. See Franklin Rasky, "Franklin and His Ladies," in *Explorers of the North: The North Pole or Bust* (Toronto: McGraw-Hill Ryerson, 1977).

23. Josephine Diebitsch-Peary, *My Arctic Journal: A Year among Ice Fields and Eskimos* (New York: Contemporary, AMS, 1975), 82. This work will be cited in the text as *MAJ*. For further reading on the Arctic explorer Adolphus W. Greely, see his autobiography, *Reminiscences of Adventure and Service* (New York: Scribner, 1927).

24. Dea Birkett, *Spinsters Abroad: Victorian Lady Explorers* (New York: Basil Blackwell, 1989).

25. For an examination of the story of Minik Wallace, who was one of six Eskimos Peary sent to the United States to be studied by Dr. Franz Boas at the American Museum of Natural History, see Kenn Harper, *Give Me My Father's Body: The Life of Minik, the New York Eskimo* (Frobisher Bay, Canada: Blacklead Books, 1986).

26. Robert E. Peary, "The Discovery of the North Pole," *National Geographic*, October 1909, 888-91.

27. Frederick Cook, "The Discovery of the North Pole," *National Geographic*, October 1909, 892-96.

28. Cook, *Attainment of the Pole*, 310.

29. Matthew Henson, *A Black Explorer at the North Pole*, reprint (Lincoln: University of Nebraska Press, 1989), 135. Originally published under the title *A Negro Explorer at the North Pole* (New York: Stokes, 1912); notice the shift in the title from *Negro* to *Black*. I use the term *Negro* in my analysis, consistent with Henson's text.

30. Since this chapter was written, a new book has appeared on this topic: S. Allen Counter, *North Pole Legacy: Black, White, and Eskimo* (Amherst: University of Massachusetts, 1991). Also, "80 Years Later and a World Away, Eskimo Sons of Explorers Meet U.S. Kin," *New York Times*, Sunday, June 7, 1987, 25; Russell W. Gibbons, "Matthew Henson: Black Explorer Used and Discarded by Peary," *New York Times*, letter to the editor, June 21, 1987, 2; "Reunion Joins North Pole Families," *Harvard University Gazette*, May 29, 1987, 1ff.; S. Allen Counter, "The Henson Family," *National Geographic*, September 1988, 422-29.

31. Herbert, "Did He Reach the Pole?" 412.

32. Davies, "New Evidence," 58.

2. NATIONAL GEOGRAPHIC SOCIETY AND MAGAZINE

1. Benedict Anderson, *Imagined Communities: Reflections on the Origin and Spread of Nationalism* (London: Verso, 1985).

2. See Andrew Parker, Mary Russo, Doris Sommer, and Patricia Yaeger, eds., *Nationalisms and Sexualities* (New York: Routledge, 1992), 1-18, for a discussion on the way this anthology expands on the relationship between sexual identities and national affililations in various historical and cultural contexts.

3. A substantial critical analysis of the emergence of the National Geographic Society and its magazine is given by Phillip Pauley, "The World and All That Is in It: The National Geographic Society, 1888-1918," *American Quarterly* 31, no. 4 (Fall 1979): 517-32. Thanks to Donna Haraway for recommending this important article for my research. This work will be cited in the text as "NGS." Since this chapter was written two new important articles have appeared by Jane Collins and Catherine Lutz on the rela-

tion between social evolutionary thought and the *Geographic*'s use of photography. See Jane Collins and Catherine Lutz's analysis on changes in *Geographic* photographic practices in the twentieth century in "Becoming America's Lens on the World: *National Geographic* in the Twentieth Century," *South Atlantic Quarterly* 91, no. 1 (Winter 1992): 161-92. Also see Catherine Lutz and Jane Collins, "The Photograph as an Intersection of Gazes: The Example of *National Geographic*," *Visual Anthropology Review* 7 (1991): 134-49.

4. C. D. B. Bryan, *The National Geographic Society: 100 Years of Adventure and Discovery* (New York: Abrams, 1987), 65.

5. Alexander Graham Bell, "The National Geographic Society," *National Geographic*, March 1912, 273.

6. See Nathan Reingold, "Definitions and Speculations: The Professionalization of Science in America in the Nineteenth Century," in Alexandra Oleson and Sanborn C. Brown, eds., *The Pursuit of Knowledge in the Early American Republic* (Baltimore: Johns Hopkins University Press, 1976), 33-69.

7. For a list of the guiding principles followed in the development of the magazine, see *National Geographic*, March 1915, 318-20.

8. Gilbert Grosvenor, "The National Geographic Society," *National Geographic*, March 1912, 24.

9. "Advertising in the Geographic Magazine is an Exact Science," *National Geographic*, May 1914, no. 25.

10. Bell, "National Geographic Society," 273.

11. Beaumont Newhall, *The History of Photography from 1839 to the Present Day* (Garden City, N.Y.: Doubleday, 1964), 17.

12. Anderson, *Imagined Communities*, 39.

13. Bell, "National Geographic Society," 273.

14. "The National Geographic Society's Notable Year," *National Geographic*, April 1920, 345.

15. Jean-Louis Baudry, "The Mask," *Afterimage* (UK), no. 5 (Spring 1974), 27.

16. William H. Taft, "Some Recent Instances of National Altruism: The Efforts of the United States to Aid the Peoples of Cuba, Puerto Rico and the Philippines," *National Geographic*, July 1907, 431.

17. C. J. Blanchard, "The Call of the West: Homes Are Being Made for Millions of People in the Arid West," *National Geographic*, May 1909, 403.

18. Mary Mills Patrick, "The Emancipation of Mohammedan Women," *National Geographic*, January 1909, 42ff.

19. Gilbert Grosvenor, "Progress of the National Geographic Society: The Reports for the Year 1912," *National Geographic*, February 1913, 253-55.

20. Phillip Fisher, "Democratic Social Space: Whitman, Melville, and the Promise of American Transparency," *Representations*, no. 24, (Fall 1988): 60.

21. Anderson, *Imagined Communities*, 30.

22. Grosvenor, "National Geographic Society," 274.

23. "The National Geographic Society and Its Magazine," *National Geographic*, January 1936, 91.

24. Bryan, *100 Years of Adventure*, 37.

25. Tom Buckley, "With the National Geographic on Its Endless Cloudless Voyage," *New York Times Magazine*, September 6, 1970.

26. Ibid.

27. Bryan, *100 Years of Adventure*, 89.

28. Advertisement for the "Santa Fe de-Luxe California Limited," *National Geographic*, October 1911, back cover.

29. Anderson, *Imagined Communities*, 16.

30. The illustration of the Scott expedition accompanied an article by Joseph Conrad, "Geography and Some Explorers," *National Geographic*, February 1924, 270. The caption reads: "Four days before his death after he had reached the South Pole and returned within 155 miles of his home base, Captain Scott wrote: "I do not regret this journey, which has shown that Englishmen can endure hardships, help one another, and meet death with as great a fortitude as ever in the past. . . . We have been willing to give our lives for this enterprise, which is in honour of our country.""

31. Matthew Henson, *A Black Explorer at the North Pole: An Autobiographic Report by the Negro Who Conquered the Top of the World with Admiral Robert E. Peary* (New York: Walker, 1969), 140.

32. See photographs from Robert E. Peary, "The Discovery of the North Pole," *National Geographic*, October 1909, 892-916.

33. Richard Evelyn Byrd, "The First Flight to the North Pole," *National Geographic*, September 1926, 358.

34. Tom Wolfe, *The Right Stuff* (New York: Bantam, 1980), 162.

3. WHITE FADE-OUT?

1. Coco Fusco, "Fantasies of Oppositionality—Reflections on Recent Conferences in Boston and New York," *Screen* 29, no. 4 (Autumn 1988): 91.

2. See bell hooks, *Yearning: Race, Gender, and Cultural Politics* (Boston: South End, 1990); Chela Sandoval, "U.S. Third World Feminism: Towards a Theory and Method of Oppositional Consciousness in the Postmodern World," *Genders* 10 (Spring 1991): 1-24; Hazel Carby, "White Women Listen! Black Feminism and the Boundaries of Sisterhood," in Centre for Contemporary Cultural Studies, *The Empire Strikes Back: Race and Racism in Seventies Britain* (London: Hutchinson, 1982), 212-35.

3. Richard Dyer, "White," *Screen* 29, no. 4 (Autumn 1988): 44. Originally appeared in Paul Gilroy, *There Ain't No Black in the Union Jack* (London: Hutchinson, 1987), 55-56.

4. It is significant that the National Geographic Society is the largest producer of documentary films in the United States. The 90-minute 1988 video, *The Explorers: A Century of Discovery*, is a National Geographic Centennial Special that aired on PBS. All references in my text are from the script of this videotape.

5. Bill Nichols would link the documentary strategies and modes deployed in this tape (the direct-address style of the Griersonian tradition and its successor, cinema verité) to an outdated documentary tradition of filmmaking used now for ads, television news, and documentary specials but not for films. See Bill Nichols, "The Voice of Documentary," *Film Quarterly* 36, no. 3 (Spring 1983): 17-30.

6. Attention has shifted in the last ten years to how issues like gender, class, race, ethnicity, and sexual orientation are part of the discourse of representation. Critical theorists, including the following, reveal how the scientist and photographer are interested agents in the production of knowledge to which they contribute: Victor Burgin, "Seeing Sense," in *The End of Art Theory: Criticism and Postmodernity* (Atlantic Highlands, N.J.: Humanities, 1986), 51-70; Jonathon Crary, "Modernizing Vision," in Hal

Foster, ed., *Vision and Visuality: Discussion in Contemporary Culture* (Seattle: Bay Press, 1988), 29-50; Donna Haraway, "Teddy Bear Patriarchy: Taxidermy in the Garden of Eden, New York City, 1908-36," in *Primate Visions: Gender, Race, and Nature in the World of Modern Science* (New York: Routledge, 1989), 26-58; Bruno Latour and Steve Woolgar, *Laboratory Life: The Social Construction of Scientific Facts* (London: Sage, 1979); Allan Sekula, "Dismantling Modernism, Reinventing Documentary (Notes on the Politics of Representation)," in *Photography against the Grain* (Halifax: Press of the Nova Scotia College of Art and Design, 1984).

7. For other critiques of how feminism, critical theory, and postcolonial discourse are aligned with a critique of positivism, see Lata Mani, *Contentious Traditions: The Debate on Sati in Colonial India, 1780-1833* (Berkeley and Los Angeles: University of California Press, 1993); Gayatri Spivak, "Can the Subaltern Speak? Speculation on Widow Sacrifice," in *Wedge*, no. 7/8 (Winter/Spring 1985): 120-30.

8. For further background on Martin and Osa Johnson see Haraway, "Teddy Bear Patriarchy," 44-45. See also the art work of Renée Green, especially her installation "VistaVision," which deals with questions of U.S. colonialism in relation to the figures of Martin and Osa Johnson (Pat Hearn Gallery, New York City, May 1991). For more information on this installation, see the following interviews with the artist: Miwon Kwon, *Emerging New Artists*, exhibition catalogue, Sala Mendoza (Caracas, Venezuela, June 1991); Donna Harkavy, *Insights: Renée Green*, exhibition catalogue, Worcester Art Museum, November 1991: 1-7.

9. For a systematic critique of this temporal relationship see Johannes Fabian, *Time and the Other: How Anthropology Makes Its Object* (New York: Columbia University Press, 1983).

10. For other studies on Western media and imperialism see Special Issue on Imperialism of Representation, The Representation of Imperialism, *Wedge*, nos. 7/8 (Winter/Spring 1985).

11. For a trenchant critique of the figure of the scientific woman in *National Geographic*, see Donna Haraway, "The Politics of Being Female," in *Primate Visions*, 279-384.

12. Also see Dian Fossey, "Making Friends with Mountain Gorillas," *National Geographic*, January 1970, 48-68; Dian Fossey, "Imperiled Giants of the Forest," *National Geographic*, April 1981, 501-23; Dian Fossey, *Gorillas in the Mist* (Boston: Houghton-Mifflin, 1983).

13. Wally Herbert, "Did Peary Reach the Pole?" *National Geographic*, September 1988, 412.

14. Kenn Harper, *Give Me My Father's Body: The Life of Minik, the New York Eskimo* (Frobisher Bay, Canada: Blacklead Books, 1986), 10-11.

15. See Booker T. Washington, "Introduction," in Henson, *Black Explorer*, reprint (Lincoln: University of Nebraska Press, 1969), xiii-xiv.

16. See Russell W. Gibbons, "Matthew Henson: Black Explorer Used and Discarded by Peary," *New York Times*, letter to the editor, June 21, 1987, 2.

17. Henson, *Black Explorer*, 136.

18. Robert Fowler, "The Negro Who Went to the Pole with Peary," *American History Illustrated* 1, no. 2 (May 1966): 49.

19. "Reunion Joins North Pole Families," *Harvard University Gazette*, May 29, 1987, 1ff.

20. S. Allen Counter, "The Henson Family," *National Geographic*, September 1988, 424.

21. Ruth Jenkins, "D.C. Admirer of Henson Visits Grave, North Pole," in *Black History Week Supplement* of the *Washington Afro-American*, February 8, 1975.

22. Robert E. Peary, *Northward over the "Great Ice": A Narrative of Life and Work along the Shores and upon the Interior Ice-Cap of Northern Greenland in the Years 1886 and 1891-9* (London: Methuen, 1898), 1:483.

23. Edward Peary Stafford, "The Peary Family," *National Geographic*, September 1988, 419.

24. Thomas Davies, *Robert E. Peary at the North Pole* (Rockville, Md.: Foundation for the Promotion of the Art of Navigation, 1989).

25. Thomas D. Davies, "New Evidence Places Peary at the Pole," *National Geographic*, January 1990, 47.

4. SCIENCE AND WRITING

1. Surgeon E. L. Atkinson, "The Finding of the Dead," in R. F. Scott, *Scott's Last Expedition: The Personal Journal of Captain R. F. Scott, R.N., C.V.O., on His Last Journey to the South Pole*, biographical introduction by Sir J. M. Barrie (New York: Dodd, Mead, 1923), 467.

2. For critical approaches on masculinities from a feminist viewpoint, see Donna Haraway, "Teddy Bear Patriarchy: Taxidermy in the Garden of Eden, New York City, 1908-1936," in *Primate Visions: Gender, Race, and Nature in the World of Modern Science* (New York: Routledge, 1989); Susan Jeffords, " 'Things Worth Dying For': Gender and the Ideology of Collectivity in Vietnam Representation," *Cultural Critique*, no. 8 (Winter 1987-88):79-104; Eve Sedgwick, *Between Men: English Literature and Male Homosocial Desire* (New York: Columbia University Press, 1985); and Klaus Theweleit, *Male Fantasies* (Minneapolis: University of Minnesota Press, 1987).

3. R. F. Scott, "Message to the Public," in *Scott's Last Expedition*, 477.

4. Atkinson, "The Finding of the Dead," 469.

5. The following is a partial listing of later editions published under the same title: 1914 (London), 1923 (London, N.Y.), 1957 (Boston), 1964 (London, N.Y.).

6. Roland Huntford, *The Last Place on Earth* (London: Hodder & Stoughton, 1979; New York: Atheneum, 1983), 524. Originally published as *Scott and Amundsen*. This work will be cited in the text and notes as *LPE*.

7. Vilhjalmur Stefansson's and other U.S. reactions to Robert Falcon Scott's death can be found in an album of newspaper clippings titled *Expedition to the South Pole 1910-1913* in the collection of the New York Public Library Annex, 521 West 43 Street, New York, N.Y.

8. For an examination of how changes in technology and culture between 1880 and World War I created new modes of understanding time and space, see Stephen Kern, *The Culture of Time and Space: 1880-1918* (Cambridge, Mass.: Harvard University Press, 1983).

9. On the history of British polar exploration see Frank Rasky, *Explorers of the North: The North Pole or Bust* (Toronto: McGraw-Hill Ryerson, 1977), 7-128. On the British historical background see Correlli Barnett, *The Collapse of British Power* (London: Methuen, 1972); Eric Hobsbawm, "Waving Flags: Nations and Nationalism," in *The Age of Empire, 1875-1914* (New York: Pantheon, 1987), 142-64; V. G. Kiernan, *The*

Lords of Humankind: Black Man, Yellow Man, and White Man in an Age of Empire (Boston: Little, Brown, 1969). On the history of the British Royal Navy see William Clowes and Clements Markham, *The Royal Navy; A History—1897-1903*. For details on Scott's career in the Royal Navy prior to his final Antarctic expedition and his rivalry with Shackleton, see Roland Huntford, *Shackleton* (New York: Fawcett, 1985); L. B. Quartermain, *South to the Pole* (Oxford: Oxford University Press, 1967).

10. Sir Clements Markham, *The Lands of Silence: A History of Arctic and Antarctic Exploration* (Cambridge: Cambridge University Press, 1921), 174.

11. Markham, *The Lands of Silence*, 174.

12. Robert Falcon Scott, C.V.O., R.N., *The Voyage of the Discovery* (London: John Murray, 1913), 1:334.

13. Immediately following Scott's death the British government raised a generous memorial fund that went toward the expenses of compiling and publishing Scott's letters, erecting a memorial statue to honor Scott in Trafalgar Square, and providing for the families of Scott and the men who died with him in Antarctica. See the following newspaper clippings from 1913 (see note 7, this chapter) for details concerning the Scott fund: *New York Times*, February 26; *New York Sun*, February 25 and March 1. For an understanding of how the Scott story continues to be considered a part of England's national heritage see L. P. Kirwan, *A History of Polar Exploration* (London: Penguin, 1962), 292. For an account of the significance of the Scott legend outside of England, see *LPE*, 528.

14. Scott, *Scott's Last Expedition*, 470.

15. Mary Pratt's, "Imperial Stylistics, 1860-1980," in *Imperial Eyes: Travel Writing and Transculturation* (London: Routledge, 1992), identifies some of the major strategies by which the British explorer Sir Richard Burton creates positions of dominance and distance in his 1860 narrative on his discovery of Lake Tanganyika. For Pratt, Burton's strategy of what she refers to as "making the home viewpoint appear normative" is one of the ways in which British exploration narratives of the period create value for their achievements in the non-West. Dean MacCannell's *The Tourist: A New Theory of the Leisure Class* (New York: Schocken, 1976) makes a similar argument about the workings of tourism. For MacCannell, tourists always place themselves at the center of the imaginary construction of the universe they create. Tourists' homes are the reference points by which they interpret the attractions that they visit (56).

16. For an examination of other British military heroes who expressed the imagination of British empire, see Martin Green, *Dreams of Adventure, Deeds of Empire* (New York: Basic), 3-27. For a comprehensive examination of how adventure played a key role in the history of Western European capitalistic societies, see Michael Nerlich, *Ideology of Adventure: Studies in Modern Consciousness, 1100-1750*, vol. 2 (Minneapolis: University of Minnesota Press, 1987).

17. Quotations from Evans's, Bowers's, and Oates's original notes appear in Roland Huntford, *Scott and Amundsen* (London: Hodder & Stoughton, 1979), 486, 489, 509 (reprinted as *LPE*). Huntford's quotations from Oates's diary are not publicly available. Bowers's final letters to his mother and sister are at the Scott Polar Research Institute, Cambridge. E. A. Wilson's *Terra Nova* diaries were published by Blandford Press, 1972.

18. See Huntford, *Scott and Amundsen*, 606. According to Huntford, the authority for Vitamin C deficiency as a cause of P.O. Evans's death is Dr. A. F. Rogers of the Department of Physiology of the University of Bristol, who has presented his findings in "The Death of Chief Petty Officer Evans," *Practitioner*, April 1974.

19. Scott, *Scott's Last Expedition*, 473.

20. Kirwan, *History of Polar Exploration*, 292.

21. Scott, *Scott's Last Expedition*, 473.

22. On the genre of tragedy see Raymond Williams, *Writing in Society* (London: Verso, 1983).

23. "The Last Place on Earth" cost Britain's Central Television 7 million pounds to produce. It was screened on British television in February 1985. The television series appeared in the United States in October 1985 and July 1988 on PBS, presented by WGBH-TV, Boston, and funded by the Mobil Corporation.

24. John Wyver, "Hero Caught in an Icy Blast," London *Times*, February 11, 1985, 12.

25. Andy Metcalf and Martin Humphries, eds., *The Sexuality of Men* (London: Pluto, 1985), 13.

26. J. Hoberman, "Vietnam: The Remake," in *Dia Art Foundation's Remaking History: Discussions in Contemporary Culture* (Seattle: Bay Press, 1989), 76.

27. See Dov Zakheim, "Is the Vietnam Syndrome Dead? Happily, It's Buried in the Gulf," *New York Times*, March 4, 1991; John Carlos Rowe, "The 'Vietnam Effect' in the Persian Gulf War," Special issue, *Cultural Critique*, no. 19 (Fall 1991), 121-50.

28. Abdul JanMohamed and Donna Przybylowicz, "Introduction: The Economy of Moral Capital in the Gulf War," Special issue, *Cultural Critique*, no. 19 (Fall 1991), 9.

29. Robert Stam, "Mobilizing Fictions: The Gulf War, the Media, and the Recruitment of the Spectator," *Public Culture* 4, 2 (Spring 1992): 117. Originally appeared in Jason de Parle, "Keeping the News in Step: Are the Pentagon's Gulf War Rules Here to Stay?" *New York Times*, May 1, 1991, 9-A.

30. See Socialist Review Bay Area Collective's article "Warring Stories: Reading and Contesting the New World Order," *Socialist Review* 21, no. 1 (January-March 1991): 11-26.

31. See Tom Wicker, "An Unknown Casualty," *New York Times*, March 20, 1991, 29-A.

32. For a more elaborate analysis of how the discourse of colonialism operated during the Gulf War, see Les Levidow, "The Gulf War as Paranoid Rationality" (Paper presented at the Dia Center for the Arts Ideologies of Technology Conference, April 12, 1992); Ella Shohat's "The Media's War," *Social Text* 9, no. 3 (1991); Edward Said, "The Arab Portrayed," *Arab World* 14, 5-7; Edward Said, "Islam through Western Eyes," *Nation*, April 26, 1980.

33. See Stam, "Mobilizing Fictions," 120-21.

34. Wicker, "An Unknown Casualty," 29-A.

Bibliography

Anthropology/Critiques of Anthropology

Clifford, James. (1988) *The Predicament of Culture*. Cambridge, Mass.: Harvard University Press.

———, and George E. Marcus, eds. (1986) *Writing Culture: The Poetics and Politics of Ethnography*. Berkeley and Los Angeles: University of California Press.

Fabian, Johannes. (1983) *Time and the Other: How Anthropology Makes Its Object*. New York: Columbia University Press.

Hulme, Peter. (1986) *Colonial Encounters*. London: Methuen.

Kiernan, V. G. (1969) *The Lords of Humankind: Black Man, Yellow Man, and White Man in an Age of Empire*. Boston: Little, Brown.

Lévi-Strauss, Claude. (1975) *Tristes Tropiques*. New York: Atheneum.

Marcus, George, and Michael Fischer. (1986) *Anthropology as Cultural Critique*. Chicago: University of Chicago Press.

Pratt, Mary Louise. (1986a) "Fieldwork in Common Places." In *Writing Culture*, edited by James Clifford and George Marcus, 27-50. Berkeley and Los Angeles: University of California Press.

———. (1986b) "Scratches on the Face of the Country; or, What Mr. Barrow Saw in the Land of the Bushmen." *Critical Inquiry* 12, no. 1: 119-43.

———. (1992) *Imperial Eyes: Travel Writing and Transculturation*. London: Routledge.

Price, Sally. (1989) *Primitive Art in Civilized Places*. Chicago: University of Chicago Press.

Rosaldo, Renato. (1989) *Culture and Truth: The Remaking of Social Analysis*. Boston: Beacon.

Cultural Criticism and Theory

Althusser, Louis. (1971) "Ideology and Ideological State Apparatuses (Notes Towards an Investigation)." In *Lenin and Philosophy*. London: Monthly Review Press.

Bibliography

Anderson, Benedict. (1985) *Imagined Communities: Reflections on the Origin and Spread of Nationalism.* London: Verso.

Auerbach, Erich. (1953) *Mimesis: The Representation of Reality in Western Literature.* Translated by Willard R. Trask. Princeton, N.J.: Princeton University Press.

Barnett, Anthony. (1982) *War Over the Falklands.* Special issue, *New Left Review,* no. 134 (July-August).

Barthes, Roland. (1972) *Mythologies.* New York: Hill & Wang.

_____. (1974) *S/Z.* New York: Hill & Wang.

_____. (1979) *The Eiffel Tower.* New York: Hill & Wang.

_____. (1982) "The Reality Effect." In *French Literary Theory Today,* edited by Tzvetan Todorov, 11-17. Cambridge: Cambridge University Press.

Baudrillard, Jean. (1983) *Simulations.* New York: Semiotext(e).

Baudry, Jean-Louis. (1974) "The Mask." *Afterimage* (UK), no. 5 (Spring).

Belsey, Catherine. (1980) "Criticism and Common Sense." In *Critical Practice.* London: Methuen.

Berger, John. (1972) *Ways of Seeing.* London: Penguin.

Bhabha, Homi. (1983) "The Other Question—The Stereotype and Colonial Discourse." *Screen* 24, no. 6: 18-36.

_____, ed. (1990) *Nation and Narration.* London: Routledge.

Boone, Joseph A. (1986) "Male Independence and the American Quest Genre: Hidden Sexual Politics in the All-Male Worlds of Melville, Twain and London." In *Gender Studies: New Directions in Feminist Criticism,* edited by Judith Specter. Bowling Green, Ohio: Bowling Green State University Popular Press.

_____, and Michael Cadden, eds. (1990) *Engendering Men: The Question of Male Feminist Criticism.* New York: Routledge.

Burgin, Victor. (1986) *The End of Art Theory: Criticism and Postmodernity.* Atlantic Highlands, N.J.: Humanities.

Conroy, Mark. (1983) "The Panoptical City: The Structure of Suspicion in *The Secret Agent.*" *Conradiana* 15, no. 3, 203-17.

Coward, Rosalind, and John Ellis. (1977) *Language and Materialism: Developments in Semiology and the Theory of the Subject.* London: Routledge and Kegan Paul.

De Certeau, Michel. (1985) "Writing the Sea: Jules Verne." In *Heterologies: Discourse on the Other.* Minneapolis: University of Minnesota Press.

Derrida, Jacques. (1974) *Of Grammatology.* Baltimore: Johns Hopkins University Press.

Dyer, Richard. (1988) "White." *Screen* 29, no. 4 (Autumn): 44-65.

Eagleton, Terry. (1983) *Literary Theory: An Introduction.* Minneapolis: University of Minnesota Press.

_____, Fredric Jameson, and Edward Said, eds. (1990) *Nationalism, Colonialism and Literature.* Minneapolis: University of Minnesota Press.

Evans, Elliott-Butler. (1989) *Race, Gender and Society: Narrative Strategies in the Fiction of Toni Cade Bambara, Toni Morrison, Alice Walker.* Philadelphia: Temple University Press.

Foster, Hal, ed. (1988) *Vision and Visuality: Discussion in Contemporary Culture.* Seattle: Bay Press.

Foucault, Michel. (1976) "The Discourse on Language." In *The Archeology of Knowledge,* 215-37. New York: Harper & Row.

Bibliography

_____. (1977) "Fantasia of the Library." In *Language, Counter-Memory, Practice*, edited by Donald Bouchard, 87-109. Ithaca, N.Y.: Cornell University Press.

_____. (1978) *Discipline and Punish*. New York: Pantheon.

_____. (1979) "What Is an Author?" In *Perspectives in Post-Structuralist Criticism*, edited by Joseph V. Harari, 27-50. Ithaca, N.Y.: Cornell University Press.

_____. (1980) "Truth and Power." In *Power/Knowledge*. New York: Pantheon.

_____. (1982) "The Subject and Power." In *Michel Foucault Beyond Structuralism and Hermeneutics*, edited by Hubert Dreyfus and Paul Rabinow, 206-26. Chicago: University of Chicago Press.

Freud, Sigmund. (1925) "The Uncanny." In *The Standard Edition of the Complete Psychological Works of Sigmund Freud*. Vol. 27. London: Hogarth.

Friedman, Lester. (1991) *Unspeakable Images: Ethnicity and the American Cinema*. Urbana: University of Illinois Press.

Giblin, Beatrice. (1977) "Geographie des mass media: La Nation-paysages 'The National Geographic Magazine.'" *Herodote*, no. 7: 148-57.

Gilman, Sander. (1985) *Difference and Pathology: Stereotypes of Sexuality, Race and Madness*. Ithaca, N.Y.: Cornell University Press.

Gilroy, Paul. (1987) *There Ain't No Black in the Union Jack: The Cultural Politics of Race and Nation*. London: Hutchinson.

Green, Martin. (1979) *Dreams of Adventure, Deeds of Empire*. New York: Basic.

Hulme, Peter. (1986) *Colonial Encounters: Europe and the Native Caribbean, 1492-1797*. New York: Methuen.

Jameson, Fredric. (1981) *The Political Unconscious: Narrative as a Socially Symbolic Act*. Ithaca, N.Y.: Cornell University Press.

_____. (1984) "Postmodernism, or the Cultural Logic of Late Capitalism." *New Left Review*, no. 11.

JanMohammed, Abdul, and Donna Przybylowicz, eds. (1991) *The Economies of War*. Special issue, *Cultural Critique*, no. 19 (Fall): 5-14.

Kauffman, L. A., and Socialist Review Bay Area Collective. (1991) *Reading and Contesting the Gulf War*. Special issue, *Socialist Review* 21, no. 1: 11-26.

MacCannell, Dean. (1976) *The Tourist: A New Theory of the Leisure Class*. New York: Schocken.

Macherey, Pierre. (1978) "Jules Verne: The Faulty Narrative." In *A Theory of Literary Production*, translated by Geoffrey Wall. London: Routledge & Kegan Paul.

Mackenzie, John, ed. (1986) *Imperialism and Popular Culture*. Manchester: Manchester University Press.

Miller, Christopher. (1985) *Blank Darkness: Africanist Discourse in French*. Chicago: University of Chicago Press.

Mosse, George L. (1985) *Nationalism and Sexuality: Middle-Class Morality and Sexual Norms in Modern Europe*. Madison: University of Wisconsin Press.

Nerlich, Michael. (1987) *Ideology of Adventure: Studies in Modern Consciousness, 1100-1750*. Vol. 2. Minneapolis: University of Minnesota Press.

Nixon, Robert. (1983) "The Alphabet and the Forces of Unreason in Woolf, Sartre, Barthes and Abish." Unpublished paper.

Pietz, William. (1987) "The Phonograph in Africa: International Phonocentrism from Stanley to Sarnoff." In *Post-Structuralism and the Question of History*, edited by Deren Attridge. Cambridge: Cambridge University Press.

Bibliography

Poirier, Richard. (1966) "Is There an I for an Eye? The Visionary Possession of America." In *A World Elsewhere: The Place of Style in American Literature*, 50-92. New York: Oxford University Press.

Poulet, Georges. (1966) *The Metamorphoses of the Circle*. Translated by Carley Dawson and Elliott Coleman. Baltimore: Johns Hopkins University Press.

Reid, Roddey. (1993) *Families in Jeopardy: Discourse, Fiction and Desire in France*. Stanford, Calif.: Stanford University Press.

Ross, Andrew. (1989) *No Respect: Intellectuals and Popular Culture*. New York: Routledge.

Rowe, John Carlos. (1991) "The 'Vietnam Effect' in the Persian Gulf War." Special issue, *Cultural Critique*, no. 19 (Fall): 121-50.

Said, Edward. (1979) *Orientalism*. New York: Vintage.

_____. (1980) "Islam through Western Eyes." *Nation*, April 26.

_____. (1983) *The World, the Text, and the Critic*. Cambridge, Mass.: Harvard University Press.

Sekula, Allan. (1984) "Dismantling Modernism, Reinventing Documentary (Notes on the Politics of Representation)." In *Photography against the Grain*, 53-76. Halifax: Press of the Nova Scotia College of Art and Design.

Selzer, Mark. (1990) "The Love Master." In *Engendering Men: The Question of Male Feminist Criticism*, edited by Joseph A. Boone and Michael Cadden, 140-58. New York: Routledge.

Serres, Michel. (1980) *Le Passage du Nord-Ouest*. Paris: Editions de Minuit.

Shohat, Ella. (1991) "The Media's War." *Social Text* (#28) 9, no. 3.

Sontag, Susan. (1977) *On Photography*. New York: Dell.

Stam, Robert. (1992) "Mobilizing Fictions: The Gulf War, the Media, and the Recruitment of the Spectator." *Public Culture* 4, no. 2: 101-26.

Todorov, Tzvetan. (1982) *The Conquest of America*. New York: Harper & Row.

Torgovnick, Marianna. (1990) *Gone Primitive: Savage Intellects, Modern Lives*. Chicago: University of Chicago Press.

White, Hayden. (1973) *Metahistory: The Historical Imagination in Nineteenth Century Europe*. Baltimore: Johns Hopkins University Press.

_____. (1978) *Tropics of Discourse: Essays in Cultural Criticism*. Baltimore: Johns Hopkins University Press.

_____. (1987) *The Content of the Form*. Baltimore: Johns Hopkins University Press.

Wieskel, Thomas. (1986) *The Romantic Sublime*. Baltimore: Johns Hopkins University Press.

Williams, Raymond. (1976) *Keywords*. New York: Oxford University Press.

_____. (1980) *Problems in Materialism and Culture*. London: Verso.

_____. (1983a) *Culture and Society 1780-1950*. New York: Columbia University Press.

_____. (1983b) *Writing in Society*. London: Verso.

Feminist Cultural Criticism, Theory, and History

Anzaldúa, Gloria, ed. (1987) *Borderlands, La Frontera: The New Mestiza*. San Francisco: Spinsters/Aunt Lute.

_____, ed. (1990) *Making Face, Making Soul: Haciendo Caras*. San Francisco: Aunt Lute.

Bibliography

Barrett, Michele, Philip Corrigan, Annette Kuhn, and Janet Wolff. (1979) "Representation and Cultural Production." In *Ideology and Cultural Production*, 9-25. New York: St. Martin's.

Barrett, Michele, ed. (1979) *Virginia Woolf: Women and Writing*. London: Women's Press.

Betterton, Rosemary, ed. (1987) *Looking On: Images of Femininity in the Visual Arts and Media*. London: Pandora.

Birkett, Dea. (1989) *Spinsters Abroad: Victorian Lady Explorers*. New York: Basil Blackwell.

Bleier, Ruth, ed. (1986) *Feminist Approaches to Science*. London: Pergamon.

Brittan, Arthur. (1989) *Masculinity and Power*. London: Basil Blackwell.

Butler, Judith. (1989) *Gender Trouble: Feminism and the Subversion of Identity*. New York: Routledge.

Caputi, Jane. (1987) *The Age of Sex Crime*. Bowling Green, Ohio: Bowling Green State University Popular Press.

Carby, Hazel. (1982) "White Women Listen! Black Feminism and the Boundaries of Sisterhood." In *The Empire Strikes Back: Race and Racism in Seventies Britain*, Centre for Contemporary Cultural Studies. London: Hutchinson.

————. (1987) *Reconstructing Womanhood*. Oxford: Oxford University Press.

Coward, Rosalind. (1985) *Female Desires: How They Are Sought, Bought and Packaged*. New York: Grove.

De Lauretis, Teresa, ed. (1986) *Feminist Studies/Critical Studies*. Bloomington: Indiana University Press.

Diamond, Irene, and Lee Quinby. (1988) *Feminism and Foucault: Reflections on Resistance*. Boston: Northeastern University Press.

Enloe, Cynthia. (1989) *Making Feminist Sense of International Politics: Bananas, Beaches, and Bases*. Berkeley and Los Angeles: University of California Press.

Franco, Jean. (1989) *Plotting Women: Gender and Representation in Mexico*. New York: Columbia University Press.

Fusco, Coco. (1988) "Fantasies of Oppositionality—Reflections on Recent Conferences in Boston and New York." *Screen* 29, no. 4 (Autumn): 80-95.

Gordon, Deborah, ed. (1988) "Introduction: Feminism and the Critique of Colonial Discourse" and "Writing Culture, Writing Feminism: The Poetics and Politics of Experimental Ethnography." Special issue, Feminism and the Critique of Colonial Discourse. *Inscriptions*. nos. 3/4:1-26.

Gordon, Linda. (1976) *Women's Body, Women's Right: A Social History of Birth Control in America*. New York: Viking.

Grosz, Elizabeth. (1989) "Sexual Difference and the Problem of Essentialism." *Inscriptions*, no. 5, 86-101.

Haraway, Donna. (1985) "A Manifesto for Cyborgs: Science, Technology and Socialist Feminism in the 1980s." *Socialist Review* 15, no. 2: 65-108.

————. (1988) "Situated Knowledges: The Science Question in Feminism and the Privilege of Partial Perspective." *Feminist Studies* 14, no. 3 (Fall): 575-99.

————. (1989) *Primate Visions: Gender, Race, and Nature in the World of Modern Science*. New York: Routledge.

Harding, Sandra. (1986) *The Science Question in Feminism*. Ithaca, N.Y.: Cornell University Press.

Heath, Stephen. (1984) *The Sexual Fix*. New York: Schocken.

Bibliography

hooks, bell. (1984) *Feminist Theory: From Margin to Center*. Boston: South End.

———. (1990) *Yearning, Race, Gender, and Cultural Politics*. Boston: South End.

Hull, Gloria, Patricia Bell Scott, and Barbara Smith, eds. (1982) *All the Women Are White, All the Blacks Are Men, but Some of Us Are Brave*. New York: Feminist Press.

Jeffords, Susan. (1987-88) " 'Things Worth Dying For': Gender and the Ideology of Collectivity in Vietnam Representation." *Cultural Critique*, no. 8, 79-104.

———. (1989) *The Remasculinization of America: Gender and the Vietnam War*. Bloomington: Indiana University Press.

Kaplan, Amy. (1990) "Romancing the Empire: The Embodiment of American Masculinity in the Popular Historical Novel of the 1890s." *American Literary History* 2, no. 4 (Winter): 659-90.

Kaplan, Caren. (1993) *Questions of Travel: Postmodernism and the Poetics of Displacement*. Minneapolis: University of Minnesota Press.

Keller, Evelyn Fox. (1985) *Reflections on Gender and Science*. New Haven, Conn.: Yale University Press.

———. (1986) "Making Gender Visible in the Pursuit of Nature's Secrets." In *Feminist Studies / Critical Studies*, edited by Teresa de Lauretis, 67-77. Bloomington: Indiana University Press.

Kolodny, Annette. (1975) *The Lay of the Land: Metaphor as Experience and History in American Life and Letters*. Chapel Hill: University of North Carolina Press.

Kuhn, Annette. (1985) *The Power of the Image: Essays on Representation and Sexuality*. London: Routledge & Kegan Paul.

Lorde, Audre. (1984) "The Master's Tools Will Never Dismantle the Master's House." In *Sister Outsider*. New York: Crossing.

McClintock, Anne. (1988) "Maidens, Maps, and Mines: The Reinvention of Patriarchy in Colonial South Africa." *South Atlantic Quarterly* 87, no. 1 (Winter): 147-92.

———. (1991) " 'No Longer in a Future Heaven': Women and Nationalism in South Africa." *Transition*, no. 51, 105-22.

Mani, Lata. (1993) *Contentious Traditions: The Debate on Sati in Colonial India, 1780-1833*. Berkeley and Los Angeles: University of California Press.

Mercer, Kobena. (1989) "Recoding Narratives of Race and Nation." *Independent* 12 (January/February): 19-26.

Metcalf, Andy, and Martin Humphries, eds. (1985) *The Sexuality of Men*. London: Pluto.

Minh-ha, Trinh. (1989) *Woman Native Other*. Bloomington: Indiana University Press.

Modleski, Tania, ed. (1986) *Studies in Entertainment: Critical Approaches to Mass Culture*. Bloomington: Indiana University Press.

Mohanty, Chandra, Ann Russo, and Lourdes Torres, eds. (1991) *Third World Women and the Politics of Feminism*. Bloomington: Indiana University Press.

Moi, Toril. (1985) *Sexual/Textual Politics: Feminist Literary Theory*. London: Methuen.

Moraga, Cherrie, and Gloria Anzaldúa, eds. (1981) *This Bridge Called My Back: Writings by Radical Women of Color*. New York: Persephone.

Mulvey, Laura. (1975) "Visual Pleasure and Narrative Cinema." *Screen* 16, no. 3: 6-18.

Ortner, Sherry. (1974) "Is Female to Male as Nature Is to Culture?" In *Women, Culture, and Society*, edited by Michele Rosaldo and Louise Lamphere, 67-87. Stanford, Calif.: Stanford University Press.

Parker, Andrew, Mary Russo, Doris Sommer, and Patricia Yaeger, eds. (1992) *Nationalisms and Sexualities*. New York: Routledge.

Bibliography

Penley, Constance, and Sharon Willis, eds. (1988) Special issues on Male Trouble. *Camera Obscura* 17/18.

Pleck, J. H. (1981) *The Myth of Masculinity*. Cambridge, Mass.: MIT Press.

Pollack, Griselda. (1987) "Artists, Mythologies and Media . . . Genius and Art History," *Screen* 21, no. 3: 57-96.

———. (1988) *Vision and Difference: Femininity, Feminism and the Histories of Art*. New York: Routledge.

Rosenberg, Rosalind. (1982) *Beyond Separate Spheres: Intellectual Roots of Modern Feminism*. New Haven, Conn.: Yale University Press.

Rubin, Gayle. (1975) "The Traffic in Women: Notes on the Political Economy of Sex." In *Toward an Anthropology of Women*, edited by Rayna Rapp Reiter, 157-210. New York: Monthly Review.

Sandoval, Chela. (1991) "U.S. Third World Feminism: Towards a Theory and Method of Oppositional Consciousness in the Postmodern World." *Genders* 10 (Spring): 1-24.

Sedgwick, Eve. (1985) *Between Men: English Literature and Male Homosocial Desire*. New York: Columbia University Press.

Segal, Lynne. (1990) *Slow Motion: Changing Masculinities, Changing Men*. New Brunswick, N.J.: Rutgers University Press.

Spivak, Gayatri. (1984/85) "Criticism, Feminism, and the Institution." *Thesis Eleven*, nos. 10/11.

———. (1985) "Three Women's Texts and a Critique of Imperialism." *Critical Inquiry* 12:243-61.

———. (1987) *In Other Worlds: Essays in Cultural Politics*. New York: Methuen.

Theweleit, Klaus. (1987, 1989) *Male Fantasies*. 2 vols. Minneapolis: University of Minnesota Press.

Walkowitz, Judith. (1980) *Prostitution and Victorian Society: Women, Class and the State*. Cambridge: Cambridge University Press.

Weed, Elizabeth, ed. (1989) *Coming to Terms: Feminism, Theory, Politics*. New York: Routledge.

Weeks, Jeffrey. (1981) *Sex, Politics and Society: The Regulation of Sexuality Since 1800*. London: Longman.

Williams, Sarah. (1987) "American Identities and Banana Republic Bodies." Paper presented at the American Anthropological Association, Chicago, November 22.

Wittig, Monique. (1981) "One Is Not Born a Woman." *Feminist Issues*, nos. 1/2 (Winter), 47-54.

Woodhull, Winnie. (1991) "Unveiling Algeria." *Genders* 10 (Spring): 112-31.

Cultural History / History of Science

Bannister, Robert. (1978) *Social Darwinism: Science and Myth in Anglo-American Social Thought*. Philadelphia: Temple University Press.

Barnett, Correlli. (1972) *The Collapse of British Power*. London: Methuen.

Black, George. (1988) *Good Neighbor: How the United States Wrote the History of Central America and the Caribbean*. New York: Pantheon.

Bradbury, Malcolm, and James McFarlane, eds. (1976) *Modernism: 1890-1930*. New York: Penguin.

Bryan, C. D. B. (1987) *The National Geographic Society: 100 Years of Adventure and Discovery*. New York: Abrams.

Bibliography

Carnegie, Andrew. (1962) *The Gospel of Wealth, and Other Timely Essays*, edited by Edward Kirkland. Cambridge, Mass.: Harvard University Press.

Dubois, W. E. Burghardt. (1877) *The Philadelphia Negro: A Social Study*. New York: Blom.

Dyer, Thomas. (1980) *Theodore Roosevelt and the Idea of Race*. Baton Rouge: Louisiana State University Press.

Graham, Loren. (1981) *Between Science and Values*. New York: Columbia University Press.

Hays, Samuel. (1959) *Conservation and the Gospel of Efficiency: The Progressive Conservation Movement, 1890-1920*. Cambridge, Mass.: Harvard University Press.

Healy, David. (1970) *US Expansionism: The Imperialist Urge in the 1890s*. Madison: University of Wisconsin Press.

Hobsbawm, Eric. (1987) *The Age of Empire, 1875-1914*. New York: Pantheon Books.

————. (1990) *Nations and Nationalisms since 1780*. Cambridge: Cambridge University Press.

Kern, Stephen. (1983) *The Culture of Time and Space: 1880-1918*. Cambridge, Mass.: Harvard University Press.

Kirchner, Walther. (1950) "Mind, Mountain, and History." *Journal of the History of Ideas* 11, no. 4: 412-47.

Latour, Bruno, and Steve Woolgar. (1979) *Laboratory Life: The Social Construction of Scientific Facts*. London: Sage.

Marcell, David. (1974) *Progress and Pragmatism: James, Dewey, Beard, and the American Idea of Progress*. Westport, Conn.: Greenwood.

Nash, Roderick. (1982) *Wilderness and the American Mind*. 3d ed. New Haven, Conn.: Yale University Press.

Noble, David. (1977) *America by Design: Science, Technology, and the Rise of Corporate Capitalism*. New York: Knopf.

Pauley, Phillip J. (1979) "The World and All That Is in It: The National Geographic Society, 1888-1918." *American Quarterly* 31, no. 4 (Fall), 517-32.

Reingold, Nathan. (1976) "Definitions and Speculations: The Professionalization of Science in America in the Nineteenth Century." In *The Pursuit of Knowledge in the Early American Republic*, edited by Alexandra Oleson and Sanburn C. Brown. Baltimore: Johns Hopkins University Press.

Roosevelt, Theodore. (1924-26) *The Works of Theodore Roosevelt*. Vol. 15. New York: Scribner.

Schivelbusch, Wolfgang. (1979) *The Railway Journey: Trains and Travel in the 19th Century*. New York: Urizen.

Seton, Ernest Thompson. (1910) *Boy Scouts of America: A Handbook of Woodcraft, Scouting and Life-craft*. New York: Doubleday.

Stafford, Barbara Maria. (1984) *Art, Science, Nature, and the Illustrated Travel Account, 1760-1940*. Cambridge, Mass.: MIT Press.

Takaki, Ronald. (1979) *Iron Cages: Race and Culture in Nineteenth Century America*. New York: Knopf.

Warren, Allen. (1986) "Citizens of the Empire: Baden Powell, Scouts and Guides, and an Imperial Ideal." In *Imperialism and Popular Culture*, edited by John M. Mackenzie. Manchester, N.H.: Manchester University Press.

Wiebe, Robert. (1967) *The Search for Order 1877-1920*. Westport, Conn.: Greenwood.

Nonfictional Accounts of Polar Expeditions:
Autobiographies, Biographies, Histories

Amundsen, Roald. (1913) *The South Pole: An Account of the Norwegian Antarctic Expedition in the "Fram," 1910-1913*. 2 vols. London: Murray.

———. (1928) *My Life as an Explorer*. New York: Doubleday.

Angell, Pauline Knickerbocker. (1964) *To the Top of the World: The Story of Peary and Henson*. Chicago: Rand McNally.

Berton, Pierre. (1988) *The Arctic Grail: The Quest for the North West Passage and the North Pole, 1818-1909*. New York: Viking.

Byrd, Richard Evelyn. (1938) *Alone*. New York: Putnam.

Cook, Frederick Albert. (1913) *My Attainment of the Pole; Being the Record of the Expedition that First Reached the Boreal Center, 1907-1909*. New York: Kennerley.

———. (1951) *Return from the Pole*. Edited by Frederick J. Pohl. New York: Pellegrini & Cudahy.

Counter, S. Allen. (1987) "The Eskimo Offspring of Matthew Henson: Harvard Scholar-Explorer Reveals Untold Story of Famed North Pole Expedition in 1909." *Ebony*, January, 50-59.

Davies, Thomas. (1989) *Robert E. Peary at the North Pole*. A Report to the National Geographic Society by the Foundation for the Promotion of the Art of Navigation. Rockville, Md.: The Foundation.

Diebitsch-Peary, Josephine. *See* Peary, Josephine Diebitsch.

Eames, Hugh. (1973) *Winner Lose All: Dr. Cook and the Theft of the North Pole*. Boston: Little, Brown.

Freeman, Andrew. (1961) *The Case for Doctor Cook*. New York: Coward-McCann.

Gibbons, Russell. (1952) *An Historical Evaluation of the Cook-Peary Controversy: A Critique of the Acceptance by History and Reference Works of the Claims of Robert E. Peary against Those of Frederick Albert Cook as to the Discovery*. Ada: Ohio Northern University.

Harper, Kenn. (1986) *Give Me My Father's Body: The Life of Minik, the New York Eskimo*. Frobisher Bay, Canada: Blacklead Books.

Henson, Matthew. (1910) "The Negro at the North Pole." *The World's Work* 19 (April): 12-25.

———. ([1912] 1989) *A Black Explorer at the North Pole*. Introduction by Susan A. Kaplan. Originally published as *A Negro Explorer at the North Pole*. New York: F. Stokes. Reprint. Lincoln: University of Nebraska Press.

Herbert, Wally. (1989) *The Noose of Laurels: Robert E. Peary and the Race to the North Pole*. London: Hodder & Stoughton.

Hunt, William. (1981) *To Stand at the Pole: The Dr. Cook-Admiral Peary North Pole Controversy*. New York: Stein & Day.

Huntford, Roland. ([1979] 1983) *The Last Place on Earth*. Originally published as *Scott and Amundsen*. London: Hodder & Stoughton. Reprint. New York: Atheneum.

———. (1987) *Shackleton*. New York: Fawcett.

MacMillan, Donald. (1934) *How Peary Reached the Pole: The Personal Story of His Assistant*. Boston: Houghton Mifflin.

Markham, Clements. (1921) *The Lands of Silence: A History of Arctic and Antarctic Exploration*. Cambridge: Cambridge University Press.

Bibliography

Mirsky, Jeanette. (1948) *To the Arctic: The Story of Northern Exploration from Earliest Times to the Present*. New York: Knopf.

Mowat, Farley. (1967) *The Polar Passion: The Quest for the North Pole*. Boston: Little, Brown.

Peary, Josephine Diebitsch. ([1893] 1975) *My Arctic Journal: A Year among Ice Fields and Eskimos*. New York: Contemporary. Reprint. New York: AMS.

Peary, Robert. (1898) *Northward over the "Great Ice": A Narrative Life and Work along the Shores and upon the Interior Ice-Cap of Northern Greenland in the Years 1886 and 1891-9*. Vols. 1 and 2. London: Methuen.

——. (1903) "The Value of Arctic Exploration." *National Geographic*, December.

——. ([1910] 1986) *The North Pole: Its Discovery in 1909 under the Auspices of the Peary Arctic Club*. New York: Stokes. Reprint. Mineola, N.Y.: Dover.

——. (1917) *Secrets of Polar Travel*. New York: Century.

Rasky, Franklin. (1977) *Explorers of the North: The North Pole or Bust*. Toronto: McGraw-Hill Ryerson.

Rawlins, Dennis. (1973) *Peary at the North Pole: Fact or Fiction?* Washington: Luce.

Scott, Robert Falcon, C.V.O., R.N. (1913) *The Voyage of the Discovery*. London: John Murray.

——. (1923) *Scott's Last Expedition: The Personal Journal of Captain R. F. Scott, R.N., C.V.O., on His Last Journey to the South Pole*. Arranged by Leonard Huxley. London: Smith, Elder.

——. (1968) *The Diaries of Captain Robert Scott*. Facsimile edition. Tylers Green, Buckinghamshire: University Microfilms.

Steger, Will, and Paul Schurke. (1987) *North to the Pole*. New York: Times Books.

Victor, Paul-Emile. (1963) *Man and the Conquest of the Poles*. New York: Simon & Schuster.

Literary Accounts of Polar Expeditions

Brody, Hugh. (1982) *Maps and Dreams*. New York: Pantheon.

——. (1987) *Living Arctic: Hunters of the Canadian North*. London: Faber & Faber.

Conrad, Joseph. (1902) *Heart of Darkness*. 2d ed. New York: Norton.

Delaney, Samuel. (1988) *Motion of Light in Water*. New York: Arbor House.

Doctorow, E. L. (1975) *Ragtime*. New York: Bantam.

Hardy, Thomas. (1891) *Tess of the D'Urbervilles*. Harmondsworth: Penguin.

Lopez, Barry. (1986) *Arctic Dreams: Imagination and Desire in a Northern Landscape*. New York: Scribner.

Norris, Frank. (1899) *A Man's Woman*. New York: Grosset & Dunlap.

Poe, Edgar Allan. (1960) *The Narrative of Arthur Gordon Pym*. New York: Hill & Wang.

Pynchon, Thomas. (1973) *Gravity's Rainbow*. New York: Bantam.

Shelley, Mary. (1818) *Frankenstein*. New York: Bantam.

Verne, Jules. (1870) *20,000 Leagues under the Sea*. New York: Scholastic.

Wolfe, Tom. (1980) *The Right Stuff*. New York: Bantam.

Woolf, Virginia. (1955) *To the Lighthouse*. San Diego: Harcourt Brace Jovanovich.

Index

Compiled by Robin Jackson

Index

Death: and *National Geographic* discourse, 76; in narrative of British heroism, 123-27

Diebitsch-Peary, Josephine, 6-7, 9-10, 38-42

Dogs: and Arctic travel, 121-22

Dyer, Richard, 83-85

Earhart, Amelia, 79

Enloe, Cynthia, x, 10, 138 n. 18, 140 n. 17

Eskimo. *See* Inuit

Explorer: changing concept of, 78-79; as passive, 80-81

Explorers: A Century of Discovery, The (video), 12-13, 58, 84-87

Falklands/Malvinas War, 130-31, 133

Feminism, 8-10

Feminist Theory: From Margin to Center (hooks), 9

Fiction: and *National Geographic*, 60

Film: documentary, 91; and exploration fantasy, 73-75. *See also* Hollywood; Television; Video

Fisher, Phillip, 69, 142 n. 20

Fossey, Dian, 93

Foucault, Michel, x, 17, 139 n. 2

Franklin, Sir John, 118-20

Fusco, Coco, 83

Gay criticism, 10-11

Gender: and narrative form, 127-29; and *National Geographic*, 57-82; social construction of, 7-9

Genre: of exploration narrative, 39-40

Geography: popularizing of, 58-61

Gilroy, Paul, 11, 84, 139 n. 21

Give Me My Father's Body: The Life of Minik, the New York Eskimo (Harper), 95-96

Goodall, Jane, 85

Gordan, Deborah, 137 n. 3

Gordan, Linda, 140 n. 20

Green, Reneé, 144 n. 8

Greenland, 27-28, 39-40, 106-7

Griffith, Trevor, 130

Grosvenor, Gilbert, 17-27, 59, 60-63, 75, 86, 107, 117; defense of nudity in *National Geographic*, 88; and narrative of Peary expedition, 20-27

Haraway, Donna, ix, xi, 10, 137 n. 3

Harper, Kenn, 95

Heart of Darkness (Conrad), 1-2

Hemming, Dr. John, 129

Henson, Matthew, 12, 13-14, 24, 45, 53, 78, 82, 85, 94-101, 106; autobiography of, 50-53; and *National Geographic*, 108-9

Herbert, Wally, 18-19, 54-55, 95, 102

Heroism: in *National Geographic* discourse, 93; metaphor of white, 76-82; and white women, 79. *See also* Robert E. Peary; Robert Falcon Scott

Hoberman, J., 132

Hollywood: and *National Geographic*, 72, 86; and rewriting of Vietnam, 132

hooks, bell, 9

Hulme, Peter, x

Huntford, Sir Roland, 13-14, 113-14, 119, 121, 125-27. *See also Scott and Amundsen*

Hussein, Saddam, 134, 135

Image: in *National Geographic* discourse, 65

Imagined Communities (Anderson), x

Immigration: and threat to masculine social hierarchy, 34

Imperialism: and *National Geographic*, 66-70. *See also* Colonialism

Inuits: as descendants of Peary and Henson, 101-6; vs. Eskimo, as term, 140 n. 4; as exotic, 53; exploitation of, 3, 10, 12, 23-24, 44-47, 94-96, 98; J. Diebitsch-Peary's observation of, 41-42

Iraq. *See* Persian Gulf War

It's a Wonderful Life (Capra), 73-75

Jameson, Fredric, x

Jeffords, Susan, x, 10, 138 n. 18

Index

Index

National Geographic Society, 17-56;
North Pole diary of, 18-19; passivity
of, 76-78; public reception of, 71;
and science, 116-17; and Theodore
Roosevelt, 33-35
Peary Arctic Club, 28-29, 32
Peary at the Pole: Fact or Fiction?
(Rawlins), 18
Persian Gulf War, 132-35
Photography: as art, 93-94; as
documentation, 55-56, 60-62, 75; and
National Geographic, 5, 12; of Peary
and Henson, 108-9; and political
rhetoric, 63-64, 67; and use of
dissolve, 87-88
Polar exploration: as metaphor for
progress, 4; as political allegory,
130-31. *See also National
Geographic*
Powell, Colin, 134
Pratt, Mary Louise, x, 146 n. 15

Race: and *National Geographic*, 57-82;
and white ethnicity, 83-85
Rain forest: colonialist view of, 92-93
Rasmussen, Knud, 28
Rawlins, Dennis, 18, 107
Return from the Pole (Cook), 28, 32
Right Stuff, The (Wolfe), 81-82
Robbins, Bruce, x
Rock, Joseph, 90-91
Romanticism: and metaphor of self-
sacrifice, 128; and nationalism, 118
Roosevelt, Franklin Delano, 32
Roosevelt, Theodore, 32, 33-35, 55
Royal Geographical Society, 129
Royal Navy: and polar exploration,
120-21
Rubin, Gayle, 8-9
Russo, Mary, x, 137 n. 3, 141 n. 2

Said, Edward, ix, 2, 137 n. 3
Sandoval, Chela, x, 143 n. 2
Schwarzkopf, Norman, 134
Science: and ideology of polar
exploration, 4-5, 11, 12-13, 23, 24,
114-16; and writing, as male, 111-35

Scott, Captain Robert Falcon, 13, 19, 76,
111-15, 121-35
Scott, Kathleen, 112, 113-14
Scott and Amundsen (Huntford), 13-14,
113, 125-27; TV series based on,
129-30
*Scott's Last Expedition: The Personal
Journal of Captain R. F. Scott, R.N.,
C.V.O., on His Last Journey to the
South Pole*, 112
Sedgwick, Eve K., 10
Segal, Lynne, x, 139 n. 19
Sekula, Allan, 144 n. 6
Selzer, Mark, 140 nn. 17, 19
Seton, Ernest Thompson, 32-33
Sexual fantasy: and *National
Geographic*, 73-76, 77, 88-90
Shohat, Ella, x, 147 n. 32
Sommer, Doris, x, 137 n. 3, 141 n. 2
South Pole: Cook's interest in, 29;
Scott's expedition to, 111-35
Space travel, 81-82
Specials (video series), 85-87
*Spinsters Abroad: Victorian Lady
Explorers* (Birkett), 41
Spivak, Gayatri, x, 144 n. 7
Stafford, Edward Peary, 102, 106-7
Stam, Robert, 147 n. 29
Stefansson, Vilhjalmur, 114-16, 128-29
Sublime: notion of, and Scott's tragedy,
128-29

Taft, William Howell, 15, 97
Technology: and Gulf War, 132-35; and
nationalism, 4; native reception of
Western, 89-90; Peary's notion of, 62;
of polar exploration, 44, 49-50,
78-81, 121-22. *See also* Photography
Television: and exploration narrative,
129-32
Tennyson, Alfred Lord, 118
Thatcher, Margaret: government of,
130-31
Theleweit, Klaus, 139 n. 19
Through the Antarctic Night (Cook), 27
To the Lighthouse (Woolf), 7-8
Turner, Frederick Jackson, 32

162

Index